A Question in Search of an Answer

371.9
G83   Greene, Roberta.
            A question in search
        of an answer.

Temple Israel Library
Minneapolis, Minn.

Please sign your full name on the above card.

Return books promptly to the Library or Temple Office.

Fines will be charged for overdue books or for damage or loss of same.

A Question in Search of an Answer

Understanding Learning Disability in Jewish Education

by
ROBERTA M. GREENE and ELAINE HEAVENRICH

with a foreword
by
DR. JANET W. LERNER

UNION OF AMERICAN HEBREW CONGREGATIONS
NEW YORK

Copyright © 1981
by the Union of American Hebrew Congregations

Library of Congress Cataloging in Publication Data

Greene, Roberta.
A question in search of an answer.

Bibliography: p.
1. Learning disabilities. 2. Jewish religious education of children.
I. Heavenrich, Elaine, joint author. II. Title.
LC4704.G73   371.9   80-18059
ISBN 0-8074-0029-7

Manufactured in the United States of America

10 9 8 7 6 5 4 3 2 1

Contents

Acknowledgments

We would like to express our gratitude to the following people, whose support and guidance enabled us to bring this book into being:

Judy Grace, special educator, whose deep concern for Jewish children with learning problems gave her the insights to advise us from the time the idea for this book first took form;

S. Rita Falk, special educator, guidance counselor, and social worker who shared with us her understanding of children with special needs;

Rabbi Rievan Slavkin, whose spiritual guidance and concern for Jewish education provided us with warm support;

Rabbi Daniel Syme, UAHC National Director of Education, who believes as deeply as we do in the need to address special needs of Jewish religious school students;

Eileen Morse and Alice Rapkin, our talented, patient, and long-suffering typists;

Michele Banker and Elaine Sinoff, colleagues who assisted in the final stages of this book;

Judy, David, and Deborah Greene and Adam Dov Heavenrich, our children, who were so understanding of our commitment to the completion of this book and who were a source of inspiration to us;

Alan Greene and Richard Heavenrich for their love and patient guidance throughout the long preparation of this book.

A special thank you to our parents and grandparents who have made Judaism a vital force in our lives.

The authors recall the memory of Roberta Greene's father, A. Solomon Menter, who provided a living example of commitment to Judaism as an integral part of life.

Roberta M. Greene
Elaine Heavenrich

Editor's Introduction

Every Jew, youth and adult alike, deserves a full and complete Jewish education as a matter of right. In recent years, we have come to understand that certain members of our community have been denied full access to their heritage, not by fiat, but rather through insensitivity to their special learning needs. Because we care, and because our eyes have been opened to a whole new frontier in Jewish education, we are pleased to bring you *A Question in Search of an Answer*. This book constitutes an effort to bring the agenda of the special-needs child before every educator, rabbi, school board, and congregational committee. It aims at sensitizing classroom teachers, parents, and Jewish professionals to the problem and the opportunity that is within our grasp. We are indebted to Roberta Greene and Elaine Heavenrich for coming forward with a concept and bringing it to fruition.

We offer special thanks to those talented educators who read the manuscript and made many valuable suggestions: to Rienne Fleischman, Gerry Gould, Jill Kirshner, Rhea Schindler, Jane Shayne, Deborah Syme, and Rabbi Steven M. Reuben; and especially to Dr. Janet W. Lerner, leader in the field of learning disabilities, who gave so freely of her time and energy to make this book a reality. Our thanks to Ralph Davis and Stuart Benick, who exerted their untiring devotion and creative skills in transforming a manuscript into a completed volume. And to Ruth Malone, for her patience and her skillful typesetting.

We hope that you will use *A Question in Search of an Answer* as a first step toward building a strong congregational program that will broaden its perspective and open new vistas in the field of Jewish studies for every Jew in our North American Jewish community.

Rabbi Daniel B. Syme, *National Director*
UAHC Department of Education

ix

Preface

Shalom.

With this book we open our eyes to a new challenge in Jewish education, the task of understanding the individual child whose needs, for one reason or another, are "different," the child who "doesn't fit the mold," the child who has come to be known in public education as "learning disabled."

It is often said that nothing is more urgent than an idea whose time has come. And indeed the time has come for us to look at, understand, and to help the child whose individual needs are different from others.

THE CHALLENGE

Jewish tradition has long stressed the importance of educating children, with a life of Torah and study prized above all. And Jewish education is in large measure responsible for preserving that special identity—the vital difference that keeps Judaism alive.

Religious school teachers, aware of the critical role they fulfill in this age-old linking of the generations, are well-versed in individual study areas of Torah, Hebrew, literature, history, ritual, and tradition. Exciting additions have been made to the curriculum to enhance and to make Judaism relevant to twentieth-century life. New dimensions have been added with the introduction of new teaching techniques and media aids.

Yet with all the advances, there is an additional concern that the religious school must address—that of the unique problems faced by those children with learning disabilities. How is Judaism going to meet this challenge?

Jewish children with learning problems must learn about their religious heritage, but in a particularly individual way. The children are not being stubborn, or difficult or lazy, as some might believe. They really *cannot* learn in ways that most others can.

How are we to understand that difference without making these children feel different? It is imperative that this question be answered, if learning disabled students are to develop and retain their Jewish identity.

Depending on whose literature you read, there are some 2-15 percent of our school-age children who may be within the learning disabled population. This means that substantial numbers of our religious school children must be accounted for. They are too vital for us to neglect their very real needs as individuals and to penalize them as Jews—simply because they have problems in learning.

WHAT THIS BOOK TRIES TO DO

This book is not a complex in-depth study of learning disability. (Such books already exist and several are recommended in the suggested readings section for your reference.) *This book is an attempt to simplify and make more readily understandable much of the complex language that surrounds (and sometimes even obscures) the child with a learning disability.*

This is not a recipe book of easy answers and sure-cures. *It is a book to help you experiment and to create a Jewish learning environment that is best for individual children.*

This book is not meant as a one-to-one tutorial guide. *This book is written to help those most concerned with Jewish education understand the uniqueness of the individual child and, as much as possible, to incorporate individual needs into the total teaching environment. It aims at helping to max-imize the child's positive experiences with religious school, the temple, and Judaism in order to maintain with pride, dignity, and love, a lifelong Jewish identity that is personally meaningful.*

WE'RE TALKING TO YOU!

Ask a Jew a question—you'll be answered with another question. This book is meant to help answer the question "How is Judaism going to embrace Jewish children with learning differences?" As it is written by Jewish authors, it will answer with another question—

How are *you* going to work with such children?

Whether parent, teacher, administrator, or rabbi, your understanding and your input are part of the answer.

There are no easy answers. If we succeed in sensitizing you to ask the right questions about individual children, you will begin to discover answers.

Chaim Potok in his book, *In the Beginning*, writes:

> ... it is as important to learn the important
> questions as it is the important answers. It is
> especially important to learn the questions to
> which there may not be good answers. We
> have to learn to live with questions....

Each child with special individual needs is a question in search of an answer.

Roberta M. Greene
Elaine Heavenrich

Foreword

by Dr. Janet W. Lerner

The field of learning disabilities has burgeoned in the past few years because it provides a fresh way to understand and to help children who are not learning as expected in a variety of areas. Parents, educators, physicians, and other professionals have welcomed this approach for children with learning disabilities and related school disorders.

The field of learning disabilities, although a relatively new one, is maturing. It is now recognized by congress, as well as all state governments, as an accepted field of special education. Programs in public schools have mushroomed in the past decade. In fact, recent federal legislation mandates that all public school classes must provide for those children who are diagnosed as learning disabled.

The perspectives and thinking of educators engaged in learning disabilities have not sufficiently expanded into Jewish education. The major emphasis thus far has been on the academic areas of reading, arithmetic, and language. However, it is readily evident to Jewish educators that many youngsters in Jewish schools are failing to learn because of learning disabilities. The symptoms and behaviors of learning disabled youngsters are manifested by a few in almost every Jewish class and are recognized by those educators attuned to the problem.

The problems of children who are having difficulty in learning in the Jewish school are too frequently handled inappropriately. They may be treated as behavior problems and consequently learn to dislike their Jewish education and Judaism. In that case, our major objective in Jewish education—building a positive identification with Judaism—is lost. In some cases children are removed from Jewish education and affiliation because of the difficulties they are encountering. These children are being deprived of an important, crucial aspect of their lives and they, too, may be lost to our Jewish people.

What is needed is a clear recognition of the learning disabilities that some children have. Some children encounter difficulties in secular school, some in religious school, and some children in both settings. What is needed is an assessment of the individual child in terms of both learning abilities and disabilities. Finally, Jewish schools must take a look at their curricular materials and methods to see how they can be changed and modified to help these children learn and develop a healthy attitude toward being a Jew.

Roberta Greene and Elaine Heavenrich have captured the learning disabilities approach to teaching and brought it into Jewish education in their book, *A Question in Search of an Answer: Understanding Learning Disability in Jewish Education*. This book is for any teacher in a Jewish religious school. It does not require previous education or training on the part of the reader either in learning disabilities or in special education. Its aim is to sensitize the Jewish educator to the child encountering learning problems. It accomplishes this task by helping the teacher understand how the child learns and by suggesting appropriate curriculum changes in Jewish education. This book is a guide for the Jewish educator to help children with learning disorders learn and enjoy the Jewish school experience.

Introduction
Focus: A Judaism of the Heart

Jews have always been the people of the book—and not just one book—many books. Wherever they went Jews carried their books with them; they spent long hours each day engaged in study, prayer, and lively argument—and all because of their dedication to the book.

Even when the unthinkable happened and their books were taken away from them, desecrated and burned, the people of the book went on. So deeply ingrained was their Judaism that, without their beloved books in their hands, they carried their books and their Judaism in their hearts. They understood their Judaism. They loved their Judaism. They lived their Judaism.

It is this living Judaism, the Judaism of the heart, that must, in this book, become our focus.

For some children the mere presence or availability of a book does not mean that the contents of that book can be read and understood. Likewise, for some children, physical presence in a religious school classroom does not mean that they understand or absorb what is going on around them. In either case, the message most certainly will not reach the heart.

Many children in religious school are in reality denied the book. There is something in their makeup that causes them to have real problems, something that causes them to function differently from those around them. *What other students can do and what all are generally expected to do, they simply cannot do. Not negativism, nor stupidity, nor lack of interest causes this behavior; rather it is an inherent inability within and of these children that is part of their individual way of functioning.*

For some this means that they cannot read. For others it may mean that they cannot write, or sit still, or even pay attention. A child may present any one or a combination of these so-called learning disabilities. Whatever the individual problem, one thing is certain: *The problem is* real, *and the child behaves in a particular way because that child* cannot *be like anyone else. The specific learning problem is part of that child's individual identity.*

We must begin by accepting a basic fact. Some children "don't fit the mold"—and there is no way we can or should attempt to squeeze them into it.

No amount of pressure by a teacher or peer can make an 11-year-old sixth grader read and understand a text if that student can only read at third- or fourth-grade level. Likewise, a youngster with a severe writing impairment literally cannot produce a legible paper.

Think what it feels like to be a third-grade child belatedly getting the idea that reading goes from left to right, and simultaneously being confronted with Hebrew going from right to left—and having to deal with both at the same time just because the curriculum says "it's time to learn Hebrew." For this student the time may not be now—it may be later. For some it may be necessary to eliminate the formal study of Hebrew altogether.

A child must not be penalized as a Jew simply because of a different pattern of learning and functioning. A child may have a learning disability, but we must not disable that student as a Jew as well.

We must always remember that the measure of today's Jewish education may not be seen until the next generation. It cannot be quantified in terms of how many lines of Hebrew a child can read, or by how rapidly Hebrew is read; it cannot be measured by how well homework is done—for some children these are impossibilities. Rather it is to be seen in a child's feelings of closeness to the temple, love of God, personal pride in belonging to this people. For this there must be a Judaism of the heart.

To attain this goal, it is necessary that we learn to deal with individual students supportively, focusing on individual strengths and abilities.

Our ultimate goal must be *to provide a Jewish background and Jewish identity which is meaningful to the individual and which will last a lifetime.*

Part I

Toward
Understanding

1

Responsibilities in Perspective

PUBLIC EDUCATION HAS BECOME INCREASINGLY AWARE OF DIF-ferences that exist among children, so much so that within recent years the field of learning disabilities has developed to help put individual differences into perspective.

Less and less frequently are children asked to be like everyone else. They are encouraged to develop as individuals within the broader structural framework of the educational system.

A major advance made possible by this interest in the individual child is the identification of children who learn and in some ways process differently from others. These children are often set apart in the eyes of their classmates, their teachers, and themselves. They are often seen by others as failures, misfits, or dumb—or more politely, as lazy or under-achievers. More importantly, they often come to see themselves as dumb, stupid, and worthless—and are perpetually defeated.

Public education has developed methods of identification, diagnosis, and treatment for these children. A child with a learning problem may now begin to find the educational environment less hostile and more understanding, and may now begin to experience some successes rather than the despair of failure.

Yet the same children who are identified in public school remain unidentified in the religious school. As a result, we all suffer painful consequences.

3

For example, a fifth-grade child may have modifications made in the public school program so that reading materials are provided at third-grade level, the level at which the student is able to perform. At the same time in religious school, there is accountability for a fifth-grade text and a penalty imposed for an inability to measure up to the work of other classmates.

The child feels a failure. The religious school teacher begins to wonder why the child is unresponsive and begins to question personal teaching adequacy. The parents find themselves in the middle. Is it the fault of the child, the teacher, the religious school, or the parent that the child is losing interest in Judaism?

Children with learning disabilities come to religious school at the end of a long, and for them, stressful public school day. Many have already experienced the pressure of feeling dumb and stupid. They are faced with the same feelings when entering religious school, but with one critical difference. They now not only sense that they are not measuring up in the eyes of their classmates and teachers, but often feel that they are not making it as Jews. Some may even wonder if they measure up in the eyes of God.

While formal education is required by law, children can, and often do, through their own devices, become *religious* school dropouts, and may eventually leave their religion altogether.

For a moment, put yourself in the place of a sixth grader with a learning problem:

> In public school as you approach adolescence, you are still faced with being somewhat awkward and clumsy in your movements. You are eager to fit in with your peers and to be one of the crowd, yet you are not well enough coordinated to excel in

sports. Academically you can handle only fourth-grade reading materials, but you are well aware that many of those around you can already handle advanced reading. For part of the day you receive some special help. While you want the tutoring, underneath it all, you are still uneasy. You can't quite overcome that feeling of being different, that something is wrong with you.

Your teachers tell you over and over again, "I know you can do better—if only you'd try harder."

By the end of the school day you are exhausted. Once again you have failed. You have not measured up. Now it is time for religious school. "Mom, do I have to go?"

Under protest you are packed off to religious school. The concepts are difficult, the books are difficult. Your English reading is embarrassing—to say nothing of the Hebrew which utterly confounds you. "Will I ever make it?" you wonder. But your teacher is wondering something else . . . . Your teacher calls your name—and calls your name again. "Pay attention! You haven't done your homework again. Everyone else did the chapter for today—but not you. It's obvious. You don't care! If you did, you'd be prepared like everybody else."

Finally one day you come home from religious school and you know what you must do. This one's going to be rough. Everything's rough. You feel you are a failure at everything. But this is one thing you can get out of. . . if you manage to make a big enough hassle. And you're becoming real good at that the older you get—making a hassle!

"Mom! Dad! I *quit*! I'm never going back!"

> You associate being a Jew and even going
> to the temple with failure, the religious
> school as just one more place where you
> can't make it. You *have to* go to public
> school—but you *don't have to* go to
> religious school.
> Did you have much of a choice?

And so the problem confronts us...demands our attention.
There had better be a choice.

Many of our Jewish children learn and perform atypically.
They exhibit learning behaviors which can cripple—educa-
tionally, emotionally, and as Jews. Because of many changes
taking place in the larger world of education, we are now able
to begin to solve the puzzle of the individual child in the
religious school, to help in the mutual adaptation of the child
to the classroom and the classroom to the individual child,
and hopefully, to pave the way for a continuing personal
commitment to a Jewish way of life.

This sixth-grade child gives us a brief glimpse of what it can
feel like to have a learning problem. But while a child lives the
problem firsthand, it is not a concern belonging to the student alone. Parents, teachers in secular school and religious
school, the rabbi—all very much care what happens. And
there are positive ways in which those in the religious educational environment may work together on behalf of the individual child.

THE RELIGIOUS SCHOOL TEACHER

No one feels as frustrated as the child, but the dedicated
religious school teacher can run a close second. The teacher,
unaware of a specific problem or a composite of problems,

may notice a child's poor performance or behavior and may pressure that child to meet the standards set for the class. The teacher may even try to help the child individually. But without specific guidelines even the best intentions and efforts can continue to frustrate both teacher and child.

The religious school teacher, aware of the awesome responsibility of influencing a student's future Jewish identity, may begin to feel a responsibility for the child's failure.

It is not long before the teacher begins to doubt and to question: "What am I doing wrong?" "Why can't I reach this child?" "Am I as good a teacher as I thought I was?" "Do I know my subject as well as I think I do?"

These feelings are logical and natural; yet once that line is crossed, once the teacher begins to feel inadequate, the child's well-being is likely to become secondary to the ego of the teacher, now on the defensive.

In such an instance, the teacher may become judgmental—"this student is lazy," "this student doesn't like me," "this kid's parents don't care," "this character just wants to disrupt the class."

To examine oneself is healthy and often revealing, but to presume inadequacy as a teacher is quite unnecessary. While the teacher may well question personal teaching ability, the answer should often be Not Guilty.

Only when the teacher identifies the problem as having separate and external causes, is it possible to begin to search for answers.

Answers? There are no answers, not unless one knows the questions to ask. So it is time to look at the child once again—but this time with a clearer focus. If papers are continually unreadable the teacher might ask "Can the student produce a paper I can read?" If a child is always in action, "Can this student sit still?" If a child does not do the homework, the teacher could ask "Can this student do the homework?'' ''Can this student follow directions?'' or ''Can this student do a simple thing like copy from the board?''

When the teacher begins to ask questions and the answers come back resoundingly, ''No, this student can't,'' then the veil begins to lift. ''No, this student can't produce a paper I can read,'' ''No, this student can't sit still,'' ''No, this student can't follow directions.'' At least some of the right questions are being asked.

''Can't, can't, can't'' is not enough. What *can* the child do? Can the child sit still for music but not for reading? Can the child understand what is seen but not what is heard? Can the child participate in and contribute to class discussions? The possible questions are endless.

Can't and *can* go hand in hand—the more important of the two is *can*. What *can* the child do?

Knowing how to look at a child, knowing what questions to ask, being willing to adapt and modify teaching strategies to meet the child's individual needs are all integral parts of the sensitized teacher. Later in chapter 4, we will discuss step-by-step guidelines for observation of children in the religious school.

For now, it is only necessary to remember that a religious school teacher is precisely that: a teacher in the religious school, a person vitally interested in the child's future. No one is asking or expecting anything other than what the title implies. It is not necessary to be a reading specialist, or a tutor, or a guidance counselor to help a child build Jewish literacy and commitment.

It is only necessary to love Judaism, to be knowledgeable in one's subject, to be sensitive and caring, to search for the right questions and to be patient in finding the answers, and to seek out and make the best use of information from other sources to better help meet the needs of individual children.

THE PARENT

No one ever said it was easy to be a parent. Add the fact of being the Jewish parent of a child with a learning problem, and the difficulties on all sides are infinitely more complex.

If anybody is in the middle, it is the parent. With problems in the home, school, playground, and religious school, their child may fit into many situations. But more than likely, there are times when their youngster *almost* makes it, but not quite.

When it comes to being a Jew, almost making it isn't good enough. An individual has to feel a personal Judaism from within, and no one can supply that feeling for another.

A parent may wish that the child's school problem could remain in the secular school. But the wise parent knows that this cannot be. It is a part of the child and must be acknowledged to others in contact with the child in the religious school.

Because of its highly personal nature, a learning problem is an extraordinarily delicate situation, and one which carries with it many emotional overtones.

It is not easy for parents to acknowledge, even to themselves, that their child has a problem—and not just a learning problem—but anything which they interpret as an imperfection in their child. To recognize it and to live with it is only the first step—to discuss it and to acknowledge it to others is quite another. While parents manage to ask help from the secular school, from doctors or other outside consultants, they are reluctant to discuss it with the religious school. In the past, parents did not provide significant information to the religious school because they felt that much of the information was highly personal and confidential. Uncertain about what would happen to their child or with the information given, they wisely exercised their prerogative. Realistically, it is just recently that religious schools have become aware that they can do something for the child with a learning problem and have made the necessary arrangements to handle such information with the confidentiality it requires.

For many parents the threat of their child's failure in secular school is the focal point. In their priorities for concern, religious school is second; only when it represents an overload on the child, do they finally speak up—and then often in confusion or in anger.

When religious school becomes a real problem, parents are faced with the worst of possible worlds—not just religious school, but Judaism as well, becomes a divisive issue in family relations, separating parents and child. In an effort to avoid tension, parents may allow withdrawal from religious school, depriving their child of what should be a positive and deeply fulfilling life experience.

However, new opportunities exist for parent-religious school interaction. Due to the extensive evaluations now possible in secular schools and elsewhere, parents are more aware of their child's difficulties and of the possibilities for help. If understanding and assistance are attainable in the secular school, then why not also in the religious school?

Although parents through individual effort or through the ACLD* have been actively concerned in secular education, they are only now ready to take the initiative in contacting the religious school, volunteering information, and asking for help for their child.

The school may contact the parents or the parents may contact the school. The important fact is that the sharing of concerns is a creative collaboration which will benefit the individual child.

---

*For information contact your local chapter or write to Association for Children with Learning Disabilities, 4156 Library Road, Pittsburgh, Pa. 15235.

THE RABBI, THE EDUCATOR, THE SCHOOL COMMITTEE

It is through the efforts and understanding of all concerned with policy making, standards, and spiritual guidelines, along with parents and teachers, that the real machinery of action can be effected: methods of communication can be set up, guidelines can be provided, and lines of co-responsibility can be drawn to maximize the child's positive experiences and to foster lasting identity with Judaism.

As we recognize the individual needs that exist among our children, so must we recognize and respect the individual differences that exist among our religious schools. There is no way that any two congregations can be alike, just as there is no way that any two children can be totally alike in their educational needs.

Our religious schools vary in goals, hours per session or per week, in teacher background (from parent-volunteers to advanced Jewish scholars), from informal chavurot to highly structured congregations. They are further differentiated by the many personalities that must interact in setting the foundations of any given school, personalities who are one step from the actual classroom, but whose sensitivities can have far-reaching effects. Each community, each congregation, each situation is unique. Yet for each, it is a time of new awareness and of new responsibilities; the possibilities are yet to be explored.

2

Who's Who

Just who is it that we are concerned about? Who is it that has educational needs that must be accounted for in recognition of individual differences?

Before we look for answers, we must first look at a class. Certain problems are readily identifiable. Those with impaired vision wear glasses; those with impaired hearing wear hearing aids. These are specific, observable medical handicaps, and teachers regularly consider preferential seating to help these children see or hear more easily. In making such simple modifications, teachers seldom stop to think twice.

But there are other problems that are not as readily apparent. Within a class there are also children who see with 20/20 vision or who hear with a full range of sound, and yet for reasons not fully understood, may not process or respond to sight or to sound accurately. Their sensory organs are intact, but sensory messages are improperly interpreted. These children misunderstand or are confused much of the time. For example, they may be able to hear directions but not be able to carry them out; they may see letters or words but not be able to read or to understand what they see. Importantly for both child and teacher, such impairments are not visible on the surface and many children, therefore, continue to operate under a hidden handicap. Teachers, for lack of understanding, continue to frustrate both children and themselves.

Not just the ability to interpret what is seen or heard may be affected. For some children, there may be impairment of motor coordination. This might be noticeable in the child's handwriting or in awkward and clumsy movements of the child's whole body. Children with learning disabilities may manifest one or several such problems.

At the same time that handicaps may lie hidden, children will present many observable behaviors in the classroom that arise out of underlying functional problems. For example, the child may be hyperactive or have a poor attention span. Such behaviors are often misunderstood, and result in the child being labeled negatively. Teachers often come to expect so-called bad behaviors. Not surprisingly, the child manages to fit this label.

However, if the teacher is sensitized in methods of child observation, a close look at the child functioning in the classroom can lead the teacher to discover a real problem that may be effectively helped.

THE MODEL CHILD

A fifth-grade teacher *may assume* that all class members can read the texts, *may assume* that all can produce the homework, *may assume* that fifth-grade children can follow directions, or at the least, *may assume* that all are able to sit still and pay attention, *if they really want to.*

It is these assumptions, these things taken for granted, that may lead to an educational environment that by its very structure excludes some children and makes it impossible for them to live up to the model expected of them.

Assumptions. Molds. Expectations. These are the traps waiting for the child with a learning problem. When the child differs from the model, or does not fulfill expectations, then performance as well as behaviors begin to create barriers that separate the child from classmates. Simply stated, the child doesn't fit the model, because the child *can't*, not because the child won't.

THE UN-MODEL ADULT

By contrast, sit in on a class of college-age adults. . .the professor is giving a lecture, and just consider what is happening in the classroom: some students are taping the lecture, some are taping and taking notes at the same time. Others are frantically writing everything the professor says while others wait to write summary notes when the topic is completed. Some copy only board notes. Some look directly at the professor's lips or face as the lecture is given, and others attend only to the paper before them. Some students may be observed repeating facts quietly to themselves. Some are in rapt attention, while others are completely disinterested. Some smoke endlessly, as others fidget and shift in their seats or actually get up and move around. A blind student takes notes in Braille. And another student, who has a highly retentive memory, takes no notes at all.

Each student, by the time of adulthood, has developed personal strategies for coping with the demands of the classroom. In this instance, the professor is using one method for all: the lecture. It is the individual student, based on cumulative experience over the years, who is continually monitoring and modifying the personal learning (intake) experience without conscious thought.

THE UN-MODEL CHILD

Most children cannot do this. They do not yet know enough about their own ways of learning and are still in the process of experimenting to make their own modifications. Those who do try are often singled out for their discrepant performance in the class. During this trial-and-error learning process they either fit the expected model and succeed, or else they become *mis*fits, and don't make it.

While the college professor is likely to expect and to accept a broad range of individual performances reflecting a range of competencies, the teacher of an elementary or religious school is generally looking for a delimited, narrowly defined response...all children in a particular third-grade group are expected to recognize and recall three new words on page 46, and are expected to be able to read page 46 aloud. Thus the children who *cannot* fulfill any one or all tasks per expectation, are set apart as failing that lesson.

Failure separates those who *can* from those who *can't*, those who *do* from those who *don't*.

This is true in the classroom, on the playground, in the family. All situations carry with them an implied model of expectation. A child is continually assessed and then either accepted or rejected by those individuals in the immediate setting. There is constant pressure from adults and peers alike.

OBSERVABLE CLASSROOM BEHAVIORS

Classroom behaviors of a given child will thus reflect:

a. the child's underlying pattern of taking in, processing, and communicating information or subject matter

b. the assumptions and expectations made about the child (the model which the child was expected to live up to—the class standard)

c. the assumptions and expectations made about the child *by others*, based upon knowledge of the child's previous performances (a revised model—smarty, class clown, dummy)

    d. the assumptions and expectations made about the child, *by the child*, based upon knowledge of past experiences and performances, plus the past *responses of others* in the environment (a revised self-image)

It may be seen that many social behaviors are secondary to the existing problem of learning disability.

In addition, in some instances the nature of the disability may be that the child misperceives the social cues or the social situation itself. In other words, there are social problems which may operate analogously to academic ones. Further, such social imperception may occur either alone or in the presence of academic learning disabilities.

With this in mind, what are some characteristics that may be exhibited by children who have learning difficulties?

1. It may appear that the student is not trying hard enough, or that the student is not grasping meaning. Frequently it may begin with a teacher feeling that something undefinable is not quite right about a student.

2. There may be a notably high activity level. The child can't seem to sit still, and is always in motion.

3. There may be lack of activity—inaction where action is anticipated.

4. Often there is much attention-seeking behavior designed to attract peers and/or teacher. This is often disruptive to the class.

5. Attention may wander or attention span may be short. The child may seem tuned-out, in another world.

6. There may be great difficulty in understanding and carrying out directions.

7. The child may be highly impulsive, and may plunge into activities with no prior thought or plan of action, often contrary to what is expected at the time.

8. On the surface, the child may appear rigid or stubborn, unwilling to shift gears, insistent on doing things in a preferred way.
9. The child may be awkward and clumsy, poorly coordinated, and may create a disturbance by bumping into things or people.
10. There may be awkwardness in holding or in manipulating pencils, art materials, etc.
11. Written work may be messy, unreadable, and filled with frequent misspellings. Written work may also be incomplete or missing altogether.
12. Large and unexplainable gaps may become evident. The child will exhibit a high performance or ability level in some areas, coupled with unexpectedly low performance in others.
13. There may be real inconsistencies in performance. What the child may do or understand one day, may be totally unattainable on another.
14. There may be frequent confusion of left and right shown in the child's total body movement, reading, and writing.

Although most anyone fits some *of the preceding descriptions at some time, a child with a learning disability is likely to display several of these characteristics, and to display them with regularity much of the time.* These characteristics form part of the child's pattern of coping and learning, seen particularly in an educational environment. *A child with a learning disability has the potential, but is not working up to that possible level of function.** A close look at behavioral characteristics may help explain much about why the child is *not* learning and not functioning adequately in the religious school.

---

*See Chapter 3 for the legal definition of learning disability.

In the religious school the classroom teacher most likely will be the one responsible for the close-up look at the child. (Later chapters deal with guidelines and mechanics for observation.) Whatever observations are made, all are valid and are well within the competency level of the adult who will just take the time to look. It is important to remember that *there is a vast difference between observing characteristic behaviors and making a diagnosis. The burden of diagnostic work does not fall on the religious school teacher.* However, what does happen, is that the input of the observant religious school teacher can form a solid basis for communication among those concerned about a child. In many instances, the teacher may be providing valuable clues to the trained professional diagnostician.

There are many reasons why a child may have a problem in learning—learning disability, low-intellect, gifted-but-unchallenged, nonmotivation, parental attitude, emotional disturbance, physical factors. Any one, or a combination, of these may apply to a specific individual.

Whatever the reason or reasons, the first step is to stand back, take a long look at the child, and without presupposition or prejudgment, simply observe the child. The same basic types of observations may be made of all children, although the resultant findings may lead to questions in varied directions.

In this book, our major focus is on the child with a learning disability. Our concern, however, extends to all children, and many other learning problems and situations are woven into the fabric of this text, just as many and varied children are woven into the tapestry of a class.

3

Coming to Terms with Terms

For those who are not specialists in the field of learning disability, terminology can be cumbersome and confusing, one more stumbling block in the way of understanding individual children. In this chapter, many commonly used terms are simply and informally discussed. To add focus, terms are grouped in relationship to each other.

With today's new laws and guidelines every attempt is made to describe the behaviors of a child, rather than to apply a label. Yet, even with the trend toward speaking of learning disabled children in everyday terms, it is still essential that there be a common ground of understanding. For *to be valid and usable, language must have meaning*. Otherwise, as has often been the case, a superficial screen of labels and jargon completely obscures the child as a person.

19

A Case in Point

Consider the following example: A religious school teacher receives information that a student is *learning disabled, hyperactive, and anxious*. But what is the report telling the teacher? Nothing that the teacher doesn't already know. The teacher has already observed that the child has a problem in classwork, exhibits much activity, and is concerned about school. The three terms—*learning disabled, hyperactive, and anxious*—may serve to show some of the complexities involved in the use of seemingly simple language.

Learning Disability can be understood as *an umbrella term for a wide variety of learning problems relating to disturbance in functional mental processes among children who are demonstrated to have potential for success, and whose performance does not reflect their possible level of ability*. This term, when used alone, is too nonspecific to add applicable information. At best it indicates that a child was evaluated and shown to have the potential to do better than at present, and that something within the child is preventing this from happening. Further, while this label has clear legal implications for qualification to receive certain types of free educational aid or related services, to the religious school teacher, it represents a designation—and nothing more.* More information is needed.

Next, the teacher reads in the report that the child is **hyperactive**. In some cases where it truly applies, an alternative and more specific neurologic term, *hyperkinetic*, may be used. The preference toward the word *hyperactive* reflects

---

*See page 24 for federal definition.

the effort to describe behavior rather than to label a child. *Hyperactive* is exactly what the term implies: overly active.

But again it is limited. Here also, more information is needed. *How* is the child overactive? Does the youngster get up and walk around? Continually swing arms and legs or tap pencils on the desk? Constantly wiggle and fall out of chairs or tip them over? Does the child's high activity level interfere with or otherwise distract or physically harm others? By itself, the word *hyperactive* points to, but does not clarify behaviors.

And then, there was the third component, *anxiety*. **Anxiety** is a term whose nonspecific nature often causes more confusion than clarity. A person suffering from an emotional state of generalized anxiety is far different from a child with a learning problem, who displays anxiety-related behaviors. A child who cannot do computation may be tense when faced with math; a child who cannot read may be equally as tense during reading. Depending on how keenly failure is felt, depending on the frustration tolerance of a youngster, *anxiety* may be either limited to a specific situation or stimulus, or generalized to the total school experience.

Nearly all children who have problems in learning may realistically be expected to demonstrate some type of anxiety behavior relating to their personal interpretation of the frustrations caused by the school experience.

When receiving a report mentioning *anxiety*, the religious school teacher must therefore be careful *not* to assume that the child is suffering a major personality disorder when the child is, in fact, displaying a realistic response to situational factors.

How then, can a report help a religious school teacher? Obviously not by surface one-word labels. However, when carefully prepared, a report can validate observations the teacher has made, provide guidelines for additional insights, and provide a framework for coping with and planning for the needs of the child.

Let us go back to just one of the preceding terms, *hyperactivity*. If the teacher were to question further or had been given a complete report, it could be seen that the diagnostician would have backed up the teacher's observation of hyperactivity. Both have made the same basic observation. However, the trained diagnostician may be able to provide the additional information that the child is always moving because of an *inability* to sit still. The child neurologically has a need to keep moving and may not be able to control this.

In such cases, the teacher now knows that all the scolding to "Sit still! Stop fidgeting! Stop wiggling around!" will lead to a continued frustrating stalemate. Depending on the relationship of additional factors, recommendations can be made to the teacher regarding ways of coping with this child in the classroom. (See Chapter 6.)

The same basic observation of high activity level could have been met with other explanations: inability to pay attention, keeping in motion for something to do; low reading level, can't keep up with the others; disinterested, unmotivated "my family doesn't care about religious school, why should I?"; emotional disturbance, need for attention.

The observation by the religious school teacher is the same—but the input from other sources is different and, in each instance, gives the teacher some understanding of underlying causes and possible direction for the future.

When Is Information Not Information?

In the previous instance, religious school personnel, had they been familiar with terminology, could have recognized that they were being given only surface labels and not substantive descriptions.

With experience and familiarity with language, religious school personnel can develop a sense of whether the information received is significant. Then they can become better attuned to *how* to question as well as to *what* questions need to be asked.

It is with this in mind that we discuss some basic terminology, beginning first with the legislation that is in effect in this area.

The purpose of presenting terms in this manner is to create an awareness of how and where these terms are likely to appear rather than to provide technical definitions.*

Not all terminology, as used in this chapter, is found in later chapters of this book. However, it is likely to appear in either conversations or reports about given children as you begin to make inquiries and observations.

A further caution is that those experienced in the field of learning disabilities often interpret or use the same terms in different ways. Be sure to ask for further information or clarification whenever and wherever necessary.

LEGISLATION AND RELATED TERMINOLOGY

According to federal legislation, Education of Handicapped Children, PL 94-142, each state must have free public education available to all handicapped students. In essence, this law is designed to help the child of normal intelligence who is not achieving in accordance with age or ability, and who displays a severe discrepancy between achievement and intellectual ability in one or more of seven designated areas relating to communication skills or mathematical abilities.

---

*For more formal and extensive explanation of terms selected here consult references at the end of this book.

> *Specific learning disability* means a disorder in one
> or more of the basic psychological processes in-
> volved in understanding or in using language,
> spoken or written, which may manifest itself in an
> imperfect ability to listen, think, speak, read,
> write, spell, or to do mathematical calculations.
> The term includes such conditions as perceptual
> handicaps, brain injury, minimal brain dysfunc-
> tion, dyslexia, and developmental aphasia. The
> term does not include children who have learning
> problems which are primarily the result of visual,
> hearing, or motor handicaps, of mental retarda-
> tion, of emotional disturbance or of environmen-
> tal, cultural, or economic disadvantage.*

A child referred with a suspected problem must have an
assessment made which consists of psychological, educational and related testing pertaining to the suspected area of
disability. The results of testing are formulated into an *Individualized Education Program* (IEP), a written plan for
meeting the child's present levels of educational performance, both long-term and short-term instructional objectives, specific services to be provided including amount of
time involved in regular educational programs, projected
time span of services to be rendered, and a mechanism for
reevaluating and monitoring progress.

One objective of this process is to determine the *Least
Restrictive Environment* (LRE) for the individual child, i.e.,
that environment which is as close to the normal classroom as
possible, and which still meets the individualized needs of the
student. It seeks to keep learning disabled students functioning in a setting with nonhandicapped students rather than to
set them apart.

---

*Source: "Education of Handicapped Children," *Federal Register*, vol. 42, no. 163
(23 August 1977).

Often this combines a percentage of time spent in a resource room with a percentage of time spent in the regular classroom.

Mainstreaming again refers to meeting the individual needs of the student within the regular classroom environment to the extent that it is in the child's best interest.

TESTING

A diagnostic work-up of a child may include psychological, educational, emotional, social, and physiological assessment as necessary depending upon the suspected area or areas of disability. It is referred to as a *psychoeducational evaluation*. It may be done by the school psychologist and the classroom teacher, or may be a composite of findings from a number of sources such as psychologist, psychiatrist, pediatrician, neurologist, optometrist, ophthalmologist, etc., along with a classroom teacher.

As the law refers to children who have normal intellectual ability, an assessment of intelligence is basic to an evaluation.

Therefore, a *psychoeducational evaluation* usually provides some measure of intellectual potential. While a number score is obtained, results are often given classification terms (Average, Superior, Low Average) rather than a number. The two IQ tests most commonly used are the Stanford-Binet and the WISC-R (Wechsler Intelligence Scale for Children-Revised).

A report could state that a child obtained an IQ score of 115 on the WISC-R, or it could state that the child tested in the high-average range on the WISC-R. From this, one might expect the child to have the *potential* to do work at grade level. However, the potential may be far different from the actual *performance* level being demonstrated by the child in the classroom.

The actual number score of 115 tells little about the child. *The most important finding of an IQ test is a profile of strengths and weaknesses.* For example, the WISC-R contains verbal tests which test language and comprehension factors, and performance tests which include such items as arranging picture sequences, copying block patterns, coding, etc. A child could perform significantly higher in one area than in another, or could test almost the same in all areas. *The test score alone in no way reflects any of this information. The profile which reflects the strengths and weaknesses is the most important and useful information to be yielded by IQ testing.*

Further, IQ scores are known to vary. The child may have had a bad day, have been rushed during testing, or may have a severe learning disability. In such cases, the child is likely to have greater potential than tests can demonstrate at that time.

What does an IQ score tell you? It only gives some idea of potential. It also tells you to read on in the report. *IQ alone is not enough.* It is just one piece of the puzzle.

Standardized achievement testing is another piece of the puzzle. The results of standardized tests give some indication of how the child is performing in relation to peers and grade level. There can be much variation in the results of local test scores as compared to national scores.

Two terms that are often used in relation to test results are *norms* and *averages.* If these are interpreted too rigidly, they can be misleading. It would be difficult to find a youngster who only tested exactly at the *norm*, or who was completely *average* in every way.

Human beings vary from person to person. Scientific data can be quantified precisely, but people cannot. It is essential to remember that not all children can do the same thing, in the same way, at the same time.

Norms and averages may appear in reports. Like IQ scores, read them and get some sense of how the child is performing—but use caution in accepting them whole.

Once testing is completed, information becomes available regarding the child's *strengths and weaknesses.* The strong areas are *abilities* or *strengths*; the *weaknesses* are referred to variously as *areas of deficit, constraints,* or *disabilities.*

Some Thoughts about Thinking

Many terms arise from the study of brain function. Like learning disability, they are most often used as umbrella terms, serving to qualify a student for a particular type of aid. They are based in medical findings and require much additional explanation if they are to be useful to the religious school. Some of these categorizing terms are *minimal brain damage* (MBD), *neurologically impaired* (NI), *perceptually handicapped, brain-injured.*

All of the above tell the religious school that the child has a neurological problem. It is no help to the religious school teacher to know the origins of the problem, whether it occurred after birth, or whether the child was born that way.

What does matter is what to do about the problem. The findings must be supported with additional information as to implications for teaching, based on the child's pattern of learning.

Two terms which are closely related here are *perception* and *cognition*. *Perception* deals with organizing and responding to incoming sensory stimuli; *cognition* refers to knowing and thinking (and thus to learning), as opposed to purely emotional or affective factors.

Any consideration of thinking and brain function must take *processing* into account. This is critical in understanding what makes a learning disabled child "disabled."

Processing refers to the interpretation the brain gives to the incoming data from the senses. Does the brain understand what the eyes see? Does the brain get meaning from what the ears hear? Does the brain respond to what the hands feel?

It is important that this be distinguished from a related, yet vastly different term, *acuity*. *Acuity* refers to the degree of accuracy with which a sensory organ functions. Do the eyes see? Do the ears hear? Do the hands feel?

It is possible to have a high degree of sensory acuity and yet to have a *processing disorder*. For example, a child who hears all tones perfectly, may not understand incoming speech. This is one kind of *auditory processing disorder*. Any sensory organ may be involved in a processing disorder.

Modality refers to the sensory pathway being used by the child for a particular activity. (Some children need to see to learn—these are sometimes referred to as "visual learners," their preferred sensory modality is sight. It is often an oversimplification to say that a child is a purely visual learner. Most people use a combination of senses rather than just one modality.)

In preparing a lesson a teacher may use different activities or strategies utilizing varying modalities to approach the same thing, rather than relying on one modality. For example, to give directions a teacher may include posters or a model to see, oral directions to hear, and demonstration models to touch and move. In this way the teacher is addressing the needs of many different students, without singling out one child because of a unique learning pattern.

The most important piece of information about a child may well be *learning style*. *Learning style* tells *how* a child learns. What does the individual need to succeed at learning? *Learning style* refers to the individual's natural preferences such as sensory modalities for learning, in addition to any other factors considered essential for maximum functioning.

Then there are some basically straightforward terms relating to the senses, either alone or in combination:

visual	to do with the eye—sight
auditory	to do with the ear—sound
tactile	to do with the skin—touch
kinasthetic	to do with the muscles— movement
haptic	to learn by touch and movement
tactile-kinasthetic	to learn by touch and movement (haptic learning)
auditory-visual	to learn by sound and sight
sensory-motor	to respond to external stimuli and to carry out action
perceptual-motor	to be able to direct purposeful motor action through inner thought, or inner interpretation of stimuli. One type of perceptual-motor activity is *eye-hand coordination.* This is the ability of the child to direct the action of the hand through the use of vision. (This could also be called *visual-motor coordination.*)

Sensory terminology is flexible and varies in terms of the needs of the child and the writer of the report. It is obvious that these terms can be combined well beyond the terminology included here.

MOVEMENT

Many terms have to do with body movement—from *gross motor* (whole body) to *fine motor* (hands and fingers) activity. They include information regarding *laterality,* the preferred side for performing an action as well as *dominance,* the commonly used term for eye- or hand-preference.

Some children may exhibit *mixed dominance* (or *unresolved mixed dominance*) which simply tells you that the child has not yet developed a clear-cut preferred side. Others will be *ambidextrous.* They will use one hand for certain activities and will change hands for other tasks.

Children with laterality problems often exhibit difficulty in *directionality,* i.e., they lack awareness of directional orientation in space and may exhibit much confusion of left/right, up/down, front/back.

It is important for a child to develop a sense of *body-image,* the perceptual awareness of one's own body, particularly in movement in space. Disturbance of body-image may cause confusion or clumsiness in movement, bumping into things, etc.

Movements themselves may be described as *ipsilateral* or *contralateral. Ipsilateral* movement refers to movement occurring on one side of the body, i.e., the right hand and right leg moving at the same time. This type of movement can cause clumsiness or imbalance.

Contralateral movement is the coordinated movement of opposite limbs, i.e., the right hand swinging forward as the left foot walks forward.

Perceptual-Motor-Training (PMT) is the process by which some children are taught to direct and control their own movements in purposeful activity. It helps establish body-image awareness, development of large and fine muscles, and physical coordination.

DEVELOPMENT

When something is related to the course of an individual's growth, it is referred to as *developmental.* For example, if speech did not develop when expected, the resulting disorder would be called *developmental aphasia.*

Developmental lag and maturational lag are terms which refer to slow or uneven patterns of growth. They refer to the level of actual performance in relation to the level of expected performance for a specific age, grade, or stage.

Closely related to development is *readiness.* For example, the child must be ready to read before reading can be learned. A child cannot be expected to learn to read before letters are known, or before focus of the eyes can be directed. *Readiness* can be physiological or experiential. Not just reading, but all new learnings require that the child be ready to learn what is being taught. In other words, a child must have the pre-requisite steps in order before a new level can be attained. Many special educational methods are specifically designed to help the child develop *readiness* for the next step in a learning process or learning sequence.

LANGUAGE AND READING TERMINOLOGY

A major area of impairment is language disability. Disorders here fall into two broad categories:

The first of these is *receptive language.* A child must be able to receive and interpret incoming language in order to understand what is going on in the environment.

The second is *expressive language,* language as a child uses it to communicate with others. A problem may occur in *expressive language* only, or may be an outgrowth of a *receptive language* disorder. In such an instance, misperception or confusion in understanding language may then manifest itself in the inability to communicate to others.

A few basic terms will go a long way in understanding children with reading problems:

Auditory blending refers to the ability to hear and combine sounds in order to build words, for example, C + A + T = CAT.

Decoding means making the correspondence between the visual written symbol and the sound or word it represents. This may be done either by sounding out a word or by recognition of a word as a whole.

Encoding is the process of putting sound or language into the written code.

Reading comprehension is an important consideration in learning disability. A child may be able to *decode,* to sound out or call out words, yet may be totally unable to tell you what's been read. Another child may mispronounce words, substitute entirely different words or sounds and yet may be able to give evidence of understanding what's been read. In many instances *reading comprehension* levels for the same child are vastly different depending on whether silent or oral reading is involved.

BEHAVIORAL TERMS

Many terms are used to describe how a child performs or behaves. These are often characteristic behaviors of children with learning disabilities (described in chapter 2).

Hyperactivity, discussed earlier in this chapter, may be gross, whole-body movements, or small repetitive movement such as footswinging or finger-tapping. *Hyperactivity* is not necessarily a constant factor. A child's hyperactivity level often varies according to the situation, depending upon the degree of excitement, frustration level, or interest in the subject.

It is important also to be aware that, in some cases, the basic observation of over-activity could be the result of a teacher's low tolerance level for movement during class. What bothers one teacher as hyperactive behavior may not concern another teacher at all.

When a child seems to plunge into activity without prethought, does things without waiting for directions, and with a seeming lack of controls, the behavior is called *impulsivity.*

In other instances, the child is locked in to what is familiar and refuses to take a chance on new situations which might produce insecurity or failure. This is called *rigidity.*

With *perseveration,* the child cannot shift gears; the child continues something after it should stop. For example, "Mamma" might be written "Mammamma," or the letter *m* might have four humps instead of two. The child may persist in continuance of some minor or major element of a word, an activity, or a whole situation.

Note: Perseveration disturbs function. It must not be confused with perseverance, which is a positive factor and related to motivation and the will to work until success is reached.

TERMS THAT APPEAR IN MULTIPLE CONTEXTS

Many frequently used terms may not appear in a singular environment. Rather they have a broad generalized meaning which becomes more specific in terms of the subject or performance area discussed. For example, *transposition* refers to an element being moved out of its proper place and being transferred to another. It can appear in many contexts: in speaking, where words are out of sequence; within a single spoken word, where sounds or syllables are out of place; in vision, where what is seen is perceived in mixed positions; in hearing, where sounds are heard incorrectly; and in motor activities, where movements are misplaced or out of sequence.

The misplacement of elements in opposite direction from the correct form is called *reversal.* This can occur in writing where letters are formed backward or where the child writes English from right-to-left on a paper; in reading English where eyes go from right-to-left, instead of from left-to-right; in speech where sounds or words may be reversed; and in following directions in reverse sequence.

Figure-ground discrimination is the ability to differentiate major elements from lesser background elements. This is important in focusing vision; in isolating spoken language from background noises of the classroom; in knowing the relative importance of various aspects of the social setting; in paying attention to focal elements without being distracted by background detail.

Motivation is the drive necessary for learning, the will to learn. In religious school, this factor assumes added importance since family attitudes are often at variance with those of the school, particularly where the child already has a problem in secular school.

Attention is the ability to sustain a focus on a situation or subject to be learned, whereas *attention span* is the length of time a pupil can remain interested and involved in an activity. It is important to note that, as with hyperactivity levels, children have varying attention spans for varying activities.

Pacing refers to helping the child or class to shift gears, to help support a child who cannot yet move along independently. (Some children need to be slowed down, and others need to be speeded up; others merely need to know what to expect and when.) Again, a child may move at one pace in one subject area or activity and have completely different pacing needs as soon as the situation changes.

Chunking applies to the *amount* of subject matter or activity the child can handle at one time. A large task may be accomplished by a child with a learning disability if the task is broken into discrete units or elements the child can handle, at a pace the child can handle, rather than as a large task the child cannot cope with. And here again the size of the chunk varies with the situation.

BUT WHAT'S IT CALLED?

Don't worry that information regarding a child may not contain an official-sounding diagnosis beyond the designation *learning disability.* That's the whole idea. The fewer the labels, and the richer the descriptions, the more helpful a report will be to the religious school teacher—and to the child.

The most important factor is to receive *meaning* about a child. If information is presented in surface labels or confusing terminology, or without supportive explanations, additional information or clarification must be requested. The religious school must ask for language used in reports to convey *real* meaning about *real* children. That is the only way to see the child who might otherwise be hidden behind a superficial screen of labels.

4

The Seeing Eye: How to Observe Children

WHAT DO WE SEE WHEN WE LOOK AT A CHILD? WHERE DO WE even begin to unravel the questions that must be answered about the individual student? What is the child telling us by classroom behaviors?

In the preceding chapter we discussed the difference between *acuity* and *process*. Likewise, when we adults look at a child do we really see that child or merely react to behavior? Do we see only what is on the surface and then fail to process what is seen? Our failure to understand what we are observing could perhaps be a reflection of our own inability as adults to have the seeing eye.

It is not necessary to be a specialist to observe children, but it does help to be sensitized to what to look for. Only when we can begin to *see* can we begin to formulate questions about a child.

A child communicates needs through behavior, and by gaining insights into how to look at behavior, we can begin to get a clearer focus on the child.

This chapter is essential to the purpose of this book, as it develops guidelines for observations. At the outset it is important to clarify the difference between *sensitization* and *diagnosis*. What we are developing here is a *sensitization*—an awareness of how and what to question, antennae, if you will—a means to be sensitive to behavioral indicators.

Diagnostic procedures and diagnostic testing, which provide the measure and substance of a child's problem, do not fall within the area of responsibility of the religious school. But *sensitization* clearly does. The sensitized religious school teacher will then have some idea of how and what to communicate to outside sources and will have greater understanding of information being provided to the religious school by those outside sources.

The following is a guide for making sensitized observations of individual children.

SOME QUESTIONS FOR CONSIDERATION

1. *What* can *the child do?*

> A student does not cause concern when performing well. Therefore, when a teacher begins to question, the student's inadequacies are in the forefront. Yet no one is all bad or totally inadequate.

> At the outset, it helps to refocus by recognizing that, while the whole process of looking at a child does define areas of difficulty, it also serves to highlight areas of strength. Keep this in mind while observing. It may help to make you more aware of subtle clues to the child's strengths which often are overshadowed by the presenting weaknesses. These strengths may be utilized later as a basis for addressing the student's problems.

2. *Is the child producing work at grade level?*

Can the student meet the expectations of the grade level in dealing with books, materials, assignments?

3. *Does the child work independently?*

Some children do not function well alone. Some may need the teacher to direct attention toward the work at hand, and others may actually need to work with other students. It is relatively easy to assess this factor. (When the teacher is expecting individual performance only, it can also be a source of potential problems.)

4. *Does the child often ask for additional help and directions?*

Following directions is a particularly difficult area for children with learning problems. What may appear to be insecurity or attention-seeking devices may, in fact, only be a child asking for what is really *necessary* to that child. For example: "What did you say?" "Can I see it again?" "Am I doing it right?" "Is this what you meant?" "Will you do it for me?"

5. *Does the child have difficulty in following directions that are given orally or in writing?*

Careful observation of a child's response to directions can be a major clue to problems. Some children must hear directions again, others need to see them again or to have them demonstrated. Others will exhibit trial-and-error behavior, seeming oblivious to directions as given.

6. *Does the child handle simple directions but experience difficulty with those involving several steps?*

> What first appears to be an imposing mountain may often be movable stone by stone. Children with learning problems often need simplification of directions. It is essential for some that directions be given in single-step units. Many children are put on overload as soon as complex directions are given.

7. *Am I constantly asking the child to redo work? If so, why?*

> Look into what the child is being expected to do. Compare the expectation with the actual performance. It may give valuable information about what the child cannot at this time be realistically expected to do. It may also yield the level of what the child *can* be expected to do.

8. *Do I feel the child would do better if more effort were put into school?*

> Many children with learning disabilities are bright and articulate and may at first "seem like everyone else." Yet their performance consistently falls below what intuition says should be expected of them. Often problems are subtle, and this surface appearance of not-trying-hard-enough may be the first real indicator that it is time to observe a child more closely.

9. *Are there large inconsistencies between performances in school?*

> Characteristic of many children with learning disabilities are wide variations in levels of perfor-

mance. Are some things done noticeably better than others? Most children do not do equally well in everything. We all have some things that we can do better than others. But with those children having learning disabilities the difference between high and low areas is often marked enough to cause concern.

10. *Does the child forget what we've just done in class or what we did last week?*

The expectation is that once a child demonstrates understanding or ability to do something, then it is reasonable to expect the child to repeat it. However, many learning disabled children are inconsistent in that what they can do on one occasion they may not be able to do on another. (This is added reinforcement to the adult's feeling that the child is not trying or is not interested.)

11. *Is behavior consistent?*

Again it's that element of inconsistency that is key. The more frustrating the expectation is to the child, the more likely the student is to exhibit an anxious or acting-out response. Behaviors may vary considerably within a class session, depending on the demands being made of the student in each new situation.

12. *Is the child able to organize?*

Children with learning disabilities are often highly disorganized in general. This may manifest itself in the disorder of a desk, chaotic placement of objects such as each of a pair of boots being left at opposite ends of a storage area, inability to follow directions, inability to plan or follow a sequence of action, often the inability to know how or where to begin an activity or work of any kind. Also thinking and speaking may reflect inability to organize ideas and language output.

13. *Does the child take much longer than others to complete assignments?*

This is another simple observation to make. If a child is *unusually* slow in relation to others in the class, it may be well to begin observing other areas of behavior.

14. *Does the child make a futile attempt at assignments or neglect them altogether?*

If a child *can't* do the assignment, there is no way the assignment will be done! A forgetful student may be a student who has a real reason to forget.

15. *Is written work handed in, but done poorly?*

Tangible evidence of disability is often seen in written work—illegibility, poor spelling, frequent erasures, incomplete content.

16. *Is there a big difference between the child's grasp of ideas as proven by oral participation, in contrast to written work?*

This can be a major clue to a child with a learning disability. A student who is an articulate contributor to class discussion may not be able to produce written work.

17. *Do you feel the child knows more than what is demonstrated in written work? Is it easier for the child to express thoughts aloud?*

    Written work may be done, but not at a level equal to that which the student exhibits orally. To more fully tap the student's knowledge it may be necessary to provide ways for the student to express ideas aloud rather than only in writing.

18. *Does the child exhibit behaviors that are potentially disturbing to others in the class?*

    Does the child fidget or move constantly? act clownish? seek attention (how)? talk constantly?

    In some instances a child is hyperactive. In other cases a child may demonstrate cover-up behaviors for inadequacies being felt. These behaviors when seen alone would not necessarily indicate a learning problem. They can be expected, however, to accompany other observations fairly frequently if the child *does* have a learning problem.

19. *Is the child able to pay attention and concentrate?*

    By itself, difficulty in this area is seen at times in every student. With a child who has a learning disability it is likely that difficulties in paying attention or in maintaining concentration will be apparent along with many other factors. While such difficulty is to be expected then, *it is wise to make careful note of the activities or circumstances under which the child* can *maintain a sustained focus.*

20. *Under what circumstances does the child's classroom behavior change markedly?*

    What kind of change in the classroom setting leads to a change in behavior? Does it occur when the child is in contact with certain children? When certain subject areas are being taught? When one subject or activity has gone on for a length of time? When directions are given? When reading is involved? When writing is necessary? When independent activities are to be pursued? The questions here could go on and on. What frequently happens is that some change in the classroom environment (social, physical, or academic) brings about a change in the student's response, thus leading to the inconsistencies discussed earlier. The ability to observe the trigger situation here could be of major significance. If such a factor is pinpointed, then at a later time, modifications can be made to intervene when a change of behavior is otherwise anticipated.

21. *Does the child function better during visual or oral presentations rather than when written output is involved?*

Some children are alert, articulate participants during reading and discussion activities, yet their behavior changes markedly when writing is necessary. Such change may be reflected in increased tension, hyperactivity, avoidance or negativism, nonfluency, incomplete work. This observation helps define areas of strength and weakness.

22. *How does the child respond to projects that involve little or no reading or writing—i.e., creative arts, dramatics, music?*

This observation is helpful in defining areas of strength that might be overlooked. Frequently children with problems in what are considered more academic areas are highly capable in creative activities. For these children the use of creative approaches might well be one of the best avenues for learning their Judaism. *Such activities require personal involvement and what the child experiences, the child will remember.* What provides a key learning experience for some learning disabled children is valuable enrichment for others.

23. *Does the child mix up sounds or whole words in English?* (e.g., expect/except; he/she; pisghetti; aminal)

It is not necessary to make detailed observations here. Such findings are often complex and form part of the diagnostic evaluation done elsewhere. For the religious school, it is sufficient to observe that this problem exists and to prevent others from ridiculing the child.

24. *Does the child mix up sounds or whole words in Hebrew?*

This is specific to the religious school and careful observation here will help in planning remedial Hebrew strategies.

Note: Some children who have no learning problems in English have considerable difficulty specific to the mastery of Hebrew with its conflicting symbols and directions.

25. *Can the child distinguish sounds that are similar?* (ƒan/ᴠan; tin/ten)

Some students cannot distinguish sounds that are closely related. They actually perceive separate sounds as identical when in fact these sounds are not. Yet most speakers assume that the child correctly hears what is said.

If a child has this problem in English, then the problem is likely also to occur in Hebrew.

26. *Can the child read and understand English texts?*

> Problems here include appropriateness of level of difficulty, the ability to read words, and the ability to get meaning from what is read. (Some children can figure out individual words but cannot understand the content of the text.)

27. *Does the child have difficulty reading the text, but easily understand the same concepts when presented orally without any reading involved?*

> This is one possible area in which the religious school teacher can overlook the child with a learning disability. The child may be performing well orally yet not completing the work requiring reading or writing. The school may expect more than the child can do and will consider this as a child who is not trying.

28. *How would you assess the child's command of English?*

> A surface observation here will do for the religious school teacher. Can the child handle the mechanics of speech and grammar, or is there apparent difficulty in using or in understanding language? Can the child express complete thoughts or complete sentences?

29. *Can the child repeat a Hebrew word or phrase that is heard?*

> Some children cannot repeat accurately what is heard. In such cases some children may do better when the spoken word is accompanied by demonstration or pictorial materials. Others may improve when the amount of auditory material is

adjusted. Some children may do better with a smaller chunk of material to repeat. It may be necessary for others to learn a single letter-sound or syllable at a time.

30. *Is Hebrew repetition made easier or more difficult if accompanied by visual presentation of the same material?*

For some students visual presentation may be a necessary aid to learning or repeating Hebrew. Yet this same factor may distract or confuse others. Careful observation will help to determine which teaching techniques are best suited to individuals in the class. One further possibility may be to group students together who learn by similar teaching strategies.

31. *Is the child able to read Hebrew adequately yet unable to write it?*

In some cases the difficulty in Hebrew may be limited to the mechanical production of symbols. This may or may not be related to a problem in writing English symbols, or in writing per se.

32. *Are Hebrew letters reversed or written incorrectly?*

Directional confusion becomes an even bigger problem for some children when faced with the mechanics of Hebrew writing. Where this is an isolated difficulty, it may be helpful to provide starting points and arrows as cues for writing. These can serve to orient the child to the direction of Hebrew writing (see chapter 9).

33. *Does the child confuse letters with similar configurations either in reading or in writing? In English? in Hebrew? in both?*

> This difficulty may be seen in confusion of m/n, b/d, א/צ ,נ/ר , etc. If the child has this problem in English, it is likely that there will be a parallel problem in Hebrew.

34. *Are letters within individual words written in correct sequence?*

> For some children, sequencing presents a problem in general; for others it may be limited to the "reversed" direction of Hebrew.

35. *Is the child confused by the right-to-left orientation of Hebrew?*

> Some children will be confused at first, but the child with a learning disability may find the directional confusion here to be a major source of frustration, particularly if the child still has problems in the left-to-right direction of English.

36. *Can I read the child's written work?*

> There is a difference between poor or careless penmanship and the inability to write or spell. A child may not be able to form letters, may reverse letters, or may totally misspell. Often there are many erasures and even holes caused by erasing or rewriting. The child is not purposely or carelessly handing in poor written work. What looks sloppy or hastily done in fact may have been laboriously worked on. If this is a real problem in English it will likely show in Hebrew as well.

37. *What* can *the child do?*

>This is no longer a question to be kept in the background. During observation some areas of real strength may have become obvious. Perhaps some things now simply appear less difficult for the child than others.

In view of all you observed, now make note of the child's strongest areas. It is time to zero in and to put the child's strengths forward.

No one has to tell a child with a learning disability that a problem exists. No one knows it better than the child. The inadequacies the child feels contribute to a defeatist self-image. The child feels inadequate and those around often expect inadequate performance. When all—including the child—expect and anticipate failure, the child is operating under a heavy burden.

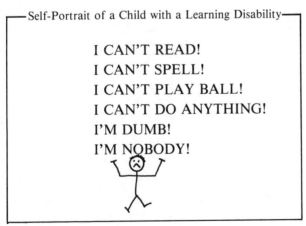

Self-Portrait of a Child with a Learning Disability

I CAN'T READ!
I CAN'T SPELL!
I CAN'T PLAY BALL!
I CAN'T DO ANYTHING!
I'M DUMB!
I'M NOBODY!

Adults often have difficulty seeing the child's strengths. Yet they are there all the time.

The child feels strengths and yet is often punished because of them. The child, deriving great satisfaction out of a creative project and glowing with success, wants to go on and on. Yet the parent or teacher sees only a strong-willed child, locked into something, and stubborn about changing activity.

Similarly, the child who cannot obtain meaning from what is said, exploring and inventing individual ways of doing things, finds that the adults in the environment treat the child as defiant, purposefully negative, and willful.

If the adults in the environment capitalized on the child's artistic strength or ability to try and try again until success is within reach, the child could feel the strengths as special and good and not detrimental.

When we can help the child to feel strengths, then our understanding can influence the self-portrait and self-image of the child with a learning problem. Then we are on the way to helping the child.

—Another Self-Portrait—

I CAN SING!
I CAN MAKE THINGS!
I CAN ADD TO A DISCUSSION!
I CAN CONTRIBUTE TO THE CLASS!
MY TEACHER UNDERSTANDS ME!
I FEEL GOOD ABOUT ME!
I COUNT!

The following checklist is offered as one means of systematically making child observations. It represents one way of answering the questions we have just discussed.

INDIVIDUAL OBSERVATION CHECKLIST FOR TEACHERS

Place check-mark next to areas which apply to child.
Double-check areas you feel are of major importance.
Comment where necessary.

Student _____

Teacher _____

Grade_____

General

_____ 1. Student is unable to keep up with work and materials used at this grade level.

_____ 2. Student does not seem to be trying.

_____ 3. Student is unable to work independently.

_____ 4. Student often asks for additional help or directions.

_____ 5. Student requires additional time to do work.

_____ 6. Student has difficulty with assignments. Are they attempted, or are they neglected altogether?

_____

_____

a. Reading assignments

_____

_____

b. Written assignments

_____

_____

_____ 7. Student's papers are done, but done poorly.

a. Handwriting_____

b. Spelling_____

c. Grammar_____

d. Have I asked student to redo work?

_____

_____ 8. Student demonstrates large inconsistencies between performances in school.

_____

_____

_____ 9. Student grasps ideas as shown by oral participation, but not as shown in written work.

_____ 10. Student has difficulty in remembering.

a. Something just explained_____

b. Something gone over last class session_____

_____ 11. Student displays awkwardness, clumsiness.

      a. _____Walking

      b. _____General incoordination of movements

      c. _____Difficulty in manipulation of writing
      materials

_____ 12. Student frequently shows confusion of left and
right.
      a. _____In reading

      b. _____In writing

      c. _____In following directions

      d. _____In moving in space

Behavior

_____ 1. Student's classroom behavior is inconsistent.
At what point is there a marked change in
behavior?

_____

_____

_____

_____ 2. Student does not seem to be able to concentrate.

_____ 3. Student exhibits short attention-span.
Under what circumstances does student show
longest attention-span?

_____

_____ 4. Student pays attention better in situations where written output is limited or is not involved.

    a. _____During visual presentations with little or no writing

    b. _____During oral presentations with little or no writing

    c. _____During creative activities with little or no writing

_____ 5. Student functions best when involved in activities with little or no reading or writing, such as creative art, dramatics, music. Describe:

_____

_____

_____ 6. Student is disorganized.

_____ 7. Student is fidgety or hyperactive. Describe:

_____

_____

_____ 8. Student is attention-seeking. How? (clowning, annoying others, etc.)

_____

_____

Socialization

_____ 1. Student is well-liked by peers.

_____ 2. Student is casually overlooked by peers.
_____ 3. Student is excluded on purpose by peers.
_____ 4. Student prefers to be alone.
_____ 5. Student prefers to be in contact with one or two others rather than in larger groups.
_____ 6. Student enters into social situations easily.
_____ 7. Student is often involved in conflict situations.

Comment_____

_____

_____

Directions
_____ 1. Student has difficulty in following oral directions.
_____ 2. Student has difficulty in following written directions.
_____ 3. Student can handle simple directions, but not those requiring many steps.
_____ 4. Student often works out own way of doing things, even when directions are given.

General Communication
1. How well does the student use language to communicate in social situations?

_____

_____

2. Does the student give complete responses or only incomplete thoughts?

_____

_____

3. Does the student seem to know more than is shown by written work?

_____

_____

_____

4. Does the student express thoughts more easily in speech or in writing?

_____

_____

_____

Language: English

_____ 1. Student has poor command of English language.
_____ 2. Student mixes up sounds or whole words in speaking. (Ex: except/expect; he/she; pisghetti; aminal)
_____ 3. Student has difficulty in hearing sounds that are similar; does not seem to distinguish closely related sounds such as *f*an/*v*an, t*i*n/t*e*n.
_____ 4. Student confuses letters or whole words that look similar. (Ex: b/d; m/n; for/from; left/felt)
_____ 5. Student cannot read and understand texts.
_____ 6. Student has difficulty with texts, but easily understands the same concepts when presented orally.
_____ 7. Student has difficulty with mechanics of writing.

a.___Letter formation   c.___Letter reversals

b.___Letter sequence   d.___Letter confusions

Language: Hebrew
_____ 1. Student cannot repeat isolated Hebrew words.
_____ 2. Student cannot repeat a Hebrew phrase.
_____ 3. Student can repeat what is heard, but cannot read or write Hebrew.
_____ 4. Is Hebrew repetition made easier or more difficult if accompanied by visual presentation of same material?

_____

_____ 5. Student can read Hebrew, but cannot write it.

_____ 6. Student mixes up sounds or whole words.

Ex: Eloheynu/Elocheynu/Elokeynu

אֱלֹהֵינוּ / אֱלֹחֵינוּ / אֱלֹכֵּינוּ

_____ 7. Student has difficulty with sounds that are similar.

Ex: ת/צ/ז/ס   כ/ק/ח

_____ 8. Student confuses letters that look similar.

Ex: א/ע/צ   ה/ח/ת   ב/כ   ג/נ   ז/ו

a. _____ In reading   b. _____ In writing

_____ 9. Student frequently reverses letters.
_____ 10. Student frequently mixes sequence of letters.
_____ 11. Student is confused by right-to-left orientation of Hebrew.

a. _____ In reading   b. _____ In writing

_____ 12. Hebrew writing is not legible.

Summary of Student's Strengths:

_____

_____

_____

_____

_____

_____

_____

Summary of Student's Weaknesses:

_____

_____

_____

_____

_____

_____

_____

5

A Question in Search of an Answer

THE TEACHER HAS SEEN, HAS QUESTIONED, AND IS NOW READY to look for some answers. But how? Where does one begin? Once one begins, where does one stop? What if there is so much information coming in that the teacher is overwhelmed? What if there is no additional help forthcoming?

At first, to an educator newly exploring the area of special needs, the amount of information regarding just one child may be intimidating. Multiply this by the number of children in any one class and the total possible amount of information is staggering.

And so the purpose of this chapter is to provide some realistic perspectives:

> No one person bears the entire burden of responsibility. No one is in it alone. This chapter discusses those who are in it together.

> While many children may be effectively helped, others may have problems too severe to be truly provided for by the religious school. It is unrealistic to ask the religious school to be all things to all people. This chapter discusses realistic expectations and limits of what may or may not be possible.

> There are wide variations in what is possible depending upon community resources, local attitudes, and the particular congregation. This chapter explores some possibilities.

There are clear-cut delineations between responsibilities of secular school education and religious school education. These distinctions are clearly made in this chapter.

The process of understanding the needs of individual children actually simplifies the situation. When a child's needs are met, the child experiences a lessening of frustration and there likely is a change in attitudes and behaviors. The teacher feels more successful as a teacher and, having provided for the child's needs, is further likely to feel a lessening of the effects of the child's frustration-related behaviors in the classroom. *What at first requires time to investigate may provide much ease in the long run.*

Jerusalem was not built in a day! Patience here is the key. Be satisfied with small—sometimes very subtle—signs of progress. The child "came equipped" with the problem. The religious school did not cause it and certainly cannot be expected to make it disappear.

The role of the religious school is to provide a continuing and positive identification with their Jewish heritage and with the temple, and to foster a love of Judaism as a way of life. That love of Judaism and warmth of understanding can be signified to and felt by the child as we make whatever modifications we can—no matter how small they may be. It requires time, patience, and much trial and error before one becomes experienced in meeting the needs of individual students with learning problems. One small step taken is far better than no step at all.

IN IT TOGETHER

Parents:
There are many reasons why parents may withhold or fail to volunteer information: fear of having their actions interpreted as those of pushy parents and then having the child

penalized for parental interference, reluctance to acknowledge the existence of the problem outside of secular school, insecurity regarding confidentiality of personal information, ignorance that the religious school is willing or is able to try to meet the needs of individuals, or simply unknowing in how to communicate such needs to the school.

The welfare of one individual is the concern of many. When the parents are aware of a problem, it is helpful for them to take the initiative in contacting the religious school. Parents often contact the person with whom they feel they can talk most comfortably—classroom teacher, principal, rabbi, or in some cases the school committee chairperson. By voluntarily informing the religious school of a problem that is already being addressed, parents are giving their child an added opportunity to find religious school a more satisfying experience, rather than one more frustration.

Teachers:

The classroom teacher probably is the first person in the religious school who will note a child with a learning problem. But being the first to see a problem does not mean that the entire responsibility rests on the teacher! The teacher must work with the principal, the parent, and with whatever additional human resources are available.

Religious School:

To assure that the teacher feels these additional supports, it is wise for the individual religious school to develop known guidelines and procedures that are flexible enough to provide for purposeful action. For parents to feel these supports, there must be some advance public relations work on the part of the school. The parent body of the school must know that the religious school welcomes this information.

A possible structure might be:

1. The teacher notes the child and observes classroom performance.

2. The teacher notifies the principal. They decide between them who should make the parental contact. Knowing the people involved ahead of time may help make the decision. For example, the classroom teacher may already know and therefore feel comfortable making personal contact and sharing concerns with some parents. The same teacher, for a number of reasons, may be less comfortable contacting others. The principal may call those parents the teacher does not feel at ease contacting. In some schools it may be standard procedure that the principal make all such *initial* contacts, while in other instances it may be optional. *In any case, the principal should be made aware of every individual problem before anyone contacts the parents.*

   Taking into consideration the child, the teacher, and the family, the essential element is that the teacher be supported and helped to do what is most comfortable in each situation.

3. Procedures must be effected to secure parental permission to contact the secular school and other sources. *It is essential that parents sign release forms before the religious school contacts any outside sources.* If, for any reason, the parent denies permission, the religious school may *not* independently consult with other sources.

4. The religious school should provide a system to insure the confidentiality of all incoming information.

Reports, as they are received from outside, should be kept in a private file in the religious school office where they may be seen by the classroom teacher. These reports should remain secured in the office. The most pertinent data may be copied for the teacher's use. If incoming data is difficult to understand, then the religious school must request clarification either in writing or by phone. (Often a learning disability consultant or a teacher is invaluable in helping to understand material sent to the religious school.)

5. Utilizing personal observations, information from parents, and information from other sources, the religious school teacher can then think through what *realistically* may be done in the individual classroom to meet the needs of the student.

LIMITS

Not every problem may be individually dealt with in the religious school. For example, severely brain damaged youngsters, severely emotionally disturbed youngsters, and mentally retarded youngsters may require extensive personalized help. Such students placed in a regular religious school classroom could drain a teacher and prevent the class from functioning.* However, many youngsters have problems which make demands upon us, but they are demands we *can* meet—unless we, by our rigidity, say it can't be done.

---

*As always, there are exceptions, and it has proven possible to meet the needs of some of these students in some classrooms.

It is our hope that every effort will be made to reach those students who, learning differences and all, may be incorporated into the flow of the regular classroom. It is our strong conviction that a modified structure and expectation will provide a maximum positive religious school experience for each Jewish child insofar as possible.

Some Possible Answers

Implementation may vary from state to state, from community to community, and from congregation to congregation.

In all states formalized legal structures exist to diagnose, designate, and help children who are learning disabled. However, funding and methods of staffing and evaluating are complex; local facilities and resources are continually reevaluated and upgraded.

Local communities and parent groups (such as the ACLD) also vary in the amount of resources and finances which are committed to children with learning problems.

In some locations learning problems are freely discussed and acknowledged while in others, in spite of the far-reaching legislation in this area, learning problems still carry the stigma of "being different."

Therefore, depending on where the religious school is located, the response to requests for information regarding individual children will vary greatly. In some communities it may be possible for a representative of the religious school to meet with secular school administrators to set guidelines for communication. In others this may not yet be possible.

Beyond the religious school, in the Jewish community-at-large, there are often philanthropic funds and Jewish family service agencies that have the human resources available to help provide for highly specialized, individual needs. Often such resources exist without our awareness of their extent, scope, and possible application to the needs of students with many kinds of severe handicaps.

Just as we must respect individual differences that exist between children, so must we respect individual differences that exist between congregations.

Within the congregation, then, what is possible? *What may be theoretically possible may be financially difficult to effect, and so the reality of what is done is knowingly often a compromise.*

Without assigning priorities to the following programs, let us examine some possibilities for placement or organization:

1. Separate Learning Disability Classes

   Some schools have set up separate classes for the *severely* learning disabled where the child spends the entire class time. However, such classes may also be asked by parents to incorporate *all* kinds of severely disabled children, and the challenge to support and staff such a class is difficult to meet.

2. Resource Room

   This is a separate room where a student may go for *part* of a religious school session to receive individualized or small group instruction. Most often this is the place for Hebrew tutorial to take place. However, a student with a substantial English language handicap could also come to this room for tutorial with someone else reading advanced or grade-level materials aloud to the child, or to work on an individualized special project related to the subject area of the entire class.

In some congregations eligibility for this kind of one-to-one tutorial depends on the established diagnosis of learning disability in secular school.

Where such programs exist for learning disabled children, it is important to also provide for the needs of those children who do not have a learning impairment but who have specific difficulty in mastering Hebrew only.

3. Teacher Aides

In some religious schools teacher aides may be available to assist in the classroom. These may be older students from the religious school, teacher trainees, or paid assistants.

4. Funding

Funding is a fact of life that cannot be escaped. Specialists cost money; special programs cost money. This is one of the very real no-win situations complicating the area of special needs. Congregations are constantly fighting the budget battle and often special education becomes the fiscal football. In public education, special education is part of the total school budget for the total educational system and no one is asked to pay extra for their individual child.

Yet in religious education parents of children with special needs are often additionally taxed. Many parents are now paying for outside diagnostic work and tutoring beyond that provided by the public school. In many cases, they are further asked to pay for special services in religious school.

5. Remedial Hebrew

This is provided to those children whose *only* difficulty is in learning Hebrew. While each congregation works to resolve the dilemma of financial responsibility for special education resources, the religious school must provide remedial Hebrew where this is the singular problem for the child. It is the specific function of a religious school to assume the responsibility for the teaching of Hebrew.

6. Teacher Sensitization

Teachers are sensitized to be alert to individual problem areas and are supported to make modifications within the regular classroom to meet specific needs of students. This can be accomplished through seminars, workshops, and in-service training.

7. Special Educator

There are several ways of utilizing the services of a special educator:

a. run separate tutorials or a resource room
b. run a special program
c. consult with teachers who question the needs of individual students at the time the problem arises
d. help coordinate and translate materials and reports sent to the religious school; help teachers map remedial classroom strategies for mainstreaming children with learning disabilities
e. help train or supervise aides to work in the classrooms along with the teachers
f. conduct training seminars for classroom teachers
g. be a liaison person with outside resources when working out the needs of a child. This function

must be carefully defined so it does not interfere with the principal's role. The special educator is *in addition to* and *not in place of* the school administration.

(In many cases a religious school may have several parents who are professionally involved in special education. While their talents may be used to support such a program, the person chosen to deal with the confidential reports must be carefully selected in order to respect the privacy of any sensitive information being shared. The paid professional special educator should, where possible, fill this function.)

8. Consultant

While it may not be possible to have a special educator *in* school, it may be possible to have an outside source who may be contacted as questions arise.

LINES OF RESPONSIBILITY

The secular school and the religious school are alike in that each accepts the responsibility for educating and caring for the individual child for a known period of time. But they are completely different in specific areas of responsibility.

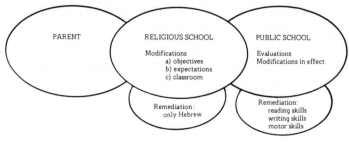

> Note that the religious school here is the inter-
> mediary between parent and secular school.
> Parents must give permission for the religious
> school to make that contact.

It is the secular school that is responsible for diagnostic
evaluation. The religious school cannot be asked to fill this
function. The only area which the religious school can and
should diagnose and remediate is that of Hebrew. All other
educational remedial work is the specific province of the
secular school.*

There is clear separation of remediation areas. *Remediation* refers to a tutorial program for specific needs. *Modification* refers to helping adjust the larger educational environment to meet the needs of individuals within the regular
classroom.

The secular school can therefore provide valuable information to the religious school regarding modifications being
made in the classroom. Many of these modifications can be
applied to the religious school. The child is already familiar
with the adaptations in secular school and might respond well
to their inclusion as part of religious education.

Establishing useful communication between the religious
school, secular school, and other consultants will take time
and effort. First attempts at obtaining and applying information may be discouraging because the concept of the religious
school wanting such information is new to many people.
There may be reluctance to share data, as well as inexperience
in communicating with persons not specifically trained in the
field of learning disability. The religious school must be clear
about what information is needed and must ask for the information in written form if it is to be used effectively. *It will*

---

*Parents may indicate other sources of information they would like the religious
school to contact instead of, or in addition to, the secular school. These might be
private consultants or outside tutors, etc.

take time, patience, and experience to develop good communication lines between the religious school and outside sources.

The religious school teacher is by no means limited to information from the secular school. Any approach or modification the religious school teacher finds successful certainly should be continued.

ADDITIONAL QUESTIONS

What if the religious school teacher observed a child, made inquiry, and found that the child was not diagnosed as having a learning problem? Some possibilities are:

a. the religious school teacher may be the first to observe a previously undiagnosed problem—the resolution of the actual diagnostic work is then up to the parent in cooperation with the secular school or other sources

b. parents may not be ready or able to acknowledge that the child has a problem

c. the religious school teacher may have found a means to help a child in the middle—a child who does not have a handicapping learning problem, but who nevertheless will benefit from individualized modifications

What if the religious school has requested cooperation from outside sources and does not receive this support or there is none available?

For whatever reason the additional input is not made, the fact remains that there is a child who

needs help. Some support is better than none at all. In this case, the religious school teacher and administration must try to adapt and be flexible however they can. Together they can try to provide that positive Jewish identity so critical to the individual child.

GATHERING INFORMATION

Each religious school must establish a specific routine for contacting outside sources. *This is to be effected only at the administrative level*; individual religious school teachers are *not* authorized to contact these sources.

The following forms are suggested for requesting data:

Release Form

Child's Name: _____

School: _____

Grade: _____

Date: _____

I hereby give _____ permission to release
                   (Name of school or consultant)

the information requested by _____
                                (Name of religious school)

regarding my child _____
                 (Name of child)

    Thank you.

               _____
                  Parent (or Guardian) Signature

Request Form

Date: _____

Name: _____
School: _____
Grade: _____

Please provide the information requested on the enclosed School Report regarding the above child. The parents (or guardians) have signed the Release form permitting you to supply this information. We would appreciate any examples of successful strategies which you are now using with this child to be described on the School Report form. Please send this information to us at your earliest convenience.

Thank you for your cooperation.

_____

Religious School Administrator

Enclosures: Release form
             School Report form

School Report

In order that we may further contact you if any questions arise, please state name and position of person completing this form.

_____
_____

Date of Report: _____

Name: _____

Grade: _____

Reading Level: _____

Writing Level: _____

Strengths:

Weaknesses:

Behavior:

Modifications in effect:

Learning style:

The following is an abbreviated checklist which the religious school teacher can use as a working guide during the process of experimenting with a variety of modifications. Teachers are encouraged to make additions and substitutions wherever necessary.

Modifications

Child's Name:_____

Seating

_____alone

_____with another child

_____in group

_____near board

_____near speaker

_____with nothing on desk except task at hand

_____private work corner

Social

_____structure social setting with known limits

_____separate from specific child/children

Organization

_____structure work

_____structure assignments

_____give single task at a time

_____check each task when done

_____help child anticipate change

_____outline sequence of events, skills, subjects

_____be patient while child gets organized

_____recognize and reward projects and assignments
worked through successfully

_____ be sure child's desk area is cleared when child is
to work there

Additional Notes

Directions
_____ requires short, one-step directions
_____ must repeat directions
_____ needs eye contact while hearing directions
_____ must see what to do (paper, page, etc.)
_____ must have demonstration
_____ must act out directions
_____ must have things to see *and* hear to
understand directions

Special Adjustments
_____ modify work load
_____ maximize oral input
_____ lessen written requirements
_____ maximize opportunities for creative
artistic expression
_____ maximize opportunities for musical
experience
_____ allow extra time to complete work
_____ reinforce what is done well
_____ make frequent eye contact with child

_____ when necessary, help child to focus
attention
_____ help child begin to speak (provide word
to start if child can't get started)
_____ provide short, varied activities
_____ allow child to move around
_____ grade constructively for content
(overlook spelling, grammar, penmanship)
_____ offer opportunity to tape-record responses
_____ give immediate feedback where child has
had successful experience
_____ make no assumptions (begin where child
is—not where class is assumed to be)

Additional Notes

The following chart may be used to give the teacher an over-view of special-needs students within a class. Vertically it provides information regarding one student at a time; horizontally it allows the teacher to see areas of need whereby certain students may require similar modifications.

All students with special needs of any kind may be incorporated into this chart.

Additional sheets may be taped to the right side of this form to create a fold-out chart to accommodate as many students as is necessary.

NOTE: This chart may be used without the vertical dividers to profile the needs of a single child.

CLASS PROFILE OF SPECIAL-NEEDS STUDENTS

NAME			
READING LEVEL			
WRITING LEVEL			
STRENGTHS			
WEAKNESSES			
MODIFICATIONS			
LEARNING STYLE			

The first half of this book is designed to lead toward understanding. It provides much of the background and tools essential to creating a living Jewish atmosphere in which the Jewish child with a learning problem may flourish as an individual.

The next half of the book implements our understandings with action.

Part II

From
Understanding
into
Action

6

Putting the Puzzle Together

IN THIS CHAPTER WE EXAMINE FOUR DIFFERENT STUDENTS IN the fifth grade, one or more of whom is likely to be found in any classroom. These are but a few examples of so-called problem children and are by no means meant as definitive of the total possible learning disabled population. For one reason or another, these students stand out and present a problem for the teacher within the framework of the classroom lesson planned. These are specific descriptions and observations that a sensitized religious school teacher can make and are taken from the checklist presented in chapter four.

We will call the students Alef, Bet, Gimel, and Dalet; the descriptions show both the strengths and the weaknesses of their learning behavior. A discussion on the parent and school input as well as specific strategies and techniques on how to deal with these four individuals follow each description.

CHILD ALEF

RELIGIOUS SCHOOL TEACHER OBSERVATIONS

Child Alef often asks the teacher, "Am I doing it right?" She needs constant reassurance that she is doing something correctly especially during independent written work. She needs to be told she is doing a good job every classroom period and needs much teacher support. Alef has a very active auditory memory. She can hear and recall accurately what has been taught or demonstrated, especially in music and rote Hebrew. When Alef has been absent and returns to class, she can recall the songs learned previously, their melodies, and the Hebrew words.

Alef often complains of a headache or stomachache when the group is reading aloud. Alef will often say, "I won't read now because I'm not feeling well." She is working below grade level in both oral reading and silent reading comprehension. She does understand what has been read to her aloud. Alef is the first to raise her hand to participate in a discussion; yet when called on she cannot respond. She cannot find a starting point to begin her answer. She will stall and use word fillers such as "Ah, ah, I know it but I can't say it" or "Oh, I forgot."

Alef interacts well in a group setting during demonstrations such as Israeli circle dancing, but if a partner-dance is taught she dominates the other child. She likes to show the other children that she knows the correct way to do it, although she often confuses her left and right when dancing.

Alef can follow oral directions well and can explain the directions to other children. Often after understanding the directions, however, she will say, "Do I have to?"

When doing written work independently, Alef monopolizes the teacher's time with questions and looks for signs of approval. Alef's writing skills are performed very well, but when accompanied with reading materials Alef will get fidgety in her seat and may complain of a stomachache.

Alef is often absent from school and the other students ask about her and want to know if she is coming back. They interact with her upon her return with questions of where she has been for so many days. Alef gives a short answer and says she was sick. Then she goes into the group and chats or plays with the others before class begins.

CONVERSATION WITH PARENTS

Alef often complains of a headache or stomachache before school, but is otherwise healthy on weekends or vacations. Her parents can't give in when it comes to public school attendance, but find it hard to insist on religious school attendance. Alef's parents seem torn between their own beliefs in the importance of religious school education and their recognition that Alef is feeling overloaded.

Alef used to need a great deal of attention from her mother. However her mother has found that a daily private time together of 15 minutes or longer leaves Alef more willing to try to become independent.

Alef is at her best when directions are given to her in simple units. ("Set the table" rather than "Set the table and feed the dog.") Parents made these adaptations as a result of suggestions from the school.

At home Alef seldom reads for enjoyment and often entertains herself with puzzles, art materials, and records, often making up songs and dances. She has neighborhood friends but has difficulty getting along with more than one child at a time.

SCHOOL REPORT

Grade: 5
Reading Level: Mid-third grade
Writing Level: Mid-third grade
Strengths
Alef has excellent auditory memory for information given in context, for rhythm and for music. She has good retention of auditory experiences.

She can participate in group discussions when context or starting point is supplied for her.

Alef is good with creative art materials and will work for long periods of time and with a feeling of success.

Weaknesses

Alef can sound out individual words but does not derive meaning from words in isolation. Alef can read for meaning at a mid-third-grade level.

She has difficulty in retaining multistep directions, particularly for written work. She can handle reading *or* writing, but is confused by more than one process.

Alef does not retain abstract or isolated directions or facts. She requires a basis for association or context and often has difficulty in beginning her answers.

Behavior

Alef has a need for teacher support and approval. When faced with reading or with complex social settings Alef exhibits a stress response of headache or stomachache. She is eager to participate but is frustrated by her own inability to read to others or to remember what she wanted to say.

MODIFICATIONS IN EFFECT

1. Directions
   Oral: Directions are given in short simple steps that are demonstrated.

   a. Alef can repeat or demonstrate her understanding of directions.

   b. Whenever possible, a visual model is provided so Alef can monitor her own responses and she can find out for herself if she is "doing it right." Alef can thus begin to become more self-reliant.

Written: Written directions are also given aloud, read by the teacher or another student. Then the same procedure as above is followed.

2. Regular time is set aside each day for private conference between teacher and student (5-10 minutes).

3. Although both reading and writing are at third-grade level, Alef has the conceptual ability anticipated for a fifth grader. She should therefore be encouraged to participate with her classmates in all areas where written materials are not involved.

4. Alef needs someone else to provide a starting point for her when she speaks before the class. This may involve providing context or shadow-speaking* when Alef is in a group discussion.

5. Allow Alef to take tests orally.

LEARNING STYLE**

Alef learns best when material is presented aloud and in context, and when accompanied by visual or action reinforcement.

---

*Actually speaking softly the first word or group of words of the answer you anticipate the child is seeking.

**This particular information may be given in a short, more complex statement such as: "Auditory input in context, accompanied by visual or kinesthetic reinforcement." While reexamination of *Modifications in Effect* may help to explain the wording it is often helpful to simply speak with the writer of the report to clarify this—or any other—information that becomes clouded by terminology. Information must be understood before it can be acted upon.

IMPLICATIONS FOR THE RELIGIOUS SCHOOL: THE TEACHER SPEAKS

How can I, as a religious school teacher, implement strategies to help this child now that I've read and absorbed the information from the parents and the public school? Now I better understand the behavior I've observed for such a long time. I recognize Alef's need for extra support and approval.

The public school states that a private five-to-ten-minute conference every day would be a step in helping Alef. But in a religious school which only meets three-to-five hours a week, a brief time once a week would be all I'd be able to give Alef privately. However, even in that time, Alef and I could discuss her work during the previous week and I could support her and help her anticipate and get ready for what will follow in the coming week. (I'll keep a small notebook for my own reference. Jotting down a word or phrase to remember about Alef would help.) Also Alef and I could develop a system of non-verbal communication which we'll use every classroom period. This could meet Alef's needs between our conferences. The system could include signals such as a smile, a wink when our eyes met, a pat on the shoulder, or a one-word statement: "Good." And these signals won't take time away from the whole class and won't set Alef apart from the others. Since she can anticipate these signals, I will meet, at least in part, her need for support.

The public school defined other modifications—such as shadow speech and visual models*—that I feel I could easily implement in the religious school classroom.

I understand from the parent that Alef feels burdened with the work she has from both schools, so I will modify her work in religious school. One way I can do this is to provide as many experiential lessons as I can [lessons based on learning materials through creating, feeling, tasting, and physical

---

*See chapter 7.

participation]. This is probably most easily done in religious school because Judaism itself provides these experiences. For written work, I can modify her assignments by lessening the output or I can ask her to read parts of chapters instead of the whole. When I'm passing out papers, no one has to know that she is only doing two questions and it can remain a private understanding between Alef and myself...but this secret may be hard to keep. When giving explanations or directions, I'll remember to give the specific references for the assignments. This will present materials and explanations in association. I won't give isolated facts because Alef won't process the information. I can lessen her reading and writing work load and allow her to concentrate and learn through music and verbal memory games.

CHILD BET

RELIGIOUS SCHOOL TEACHER OBSERVATIONS

Child Bet is representative of the hyperactive child. This kind of behavior can be seen in the classroom during every period. He cannot sit still, his arms, hands, toes, or legs are always tapping, moving, swinging—he is so fidgety he calls attention to himself. Bet is often unaware that he is doing this. He often needs to be reminded to get back to work, especially during independent written work when he will get up and walk to the window. During independent reading work, however, he does very well. He can retain information he has read and actively seeks out more information on a subject in the library. He enjoys sharing information orally with his classmates but cannot structure output and has difficulty knowing how to stop. He will ramble on and on with his wealth of information and knowledge until his classmates become bored. When it is someone else's turn to be at the center of attention, Bet has difficulty concentrating and the person sitting next to him will often be the recipient of touching, hair pulling, or poking with fingers.

Bet does his written work poorly and will say "I can't do it!" Bet understands the oral directions and written directions and will begin a written project but is easily distracted and may not complete what he has begun. What is done is done sloppily. Yet it is obvious how hard Bet is trying. He seems to have difficulty even in holding a pencil. Writing requires great effort and seems to exhaust him. Bet has difficulty spacing words and sentences on the paper. There are so many erasures his papers often have holes in them. His desk is disorganized so that pencils and books often fall on the floor. He exhibits general clumsiness.

Bet is a fast reader and communicates what he has read to others. The other students seem surprised that he can do so well in this area. Bet is highly responsive to praise from the teacher. When participating in a classroom discussion, he dominates and monopolizes time by talking at length and constantly adding more and more information. He will often interrupt another student to continue his answer.

Conversation with Parents

Bet has always been hyperactive—all over and into everything. Physically and mentally he is a challenging child to live with. He is clumsy and poorly coordinated, often spilling or bumping into things or people. He never seems to know what to do with all his energy.

He does not write or draw for amusement. Bet talks all the time and is full of questions. Fortunately he loves to read and can read for information as well as for enjoyment. He especially likes history and biography. His parents note that even when he is reading Bet is always tapping a foot or fidgeting and seems unaware of it.

Bet is curious about how things work and often takes things apart and puts them back together. Although such activity is laborious for him, Bet will persist until he is satisfied he has it right.

Bet loves biking and physical activity, but doesn't do well in sports where coordination or teamwork is required. He complains that recess and gym are getting harder for him and that the other boys pick on him.

SCHOOL REPORT
Grade: 5
Reading Level: Sixth to seventh grade
Writing Level: Third grade
Strengths

Bet's greatest asset is his intellectual curiosity and superior ability as tested on the Stanford-Binet. He is eager to seek out and share information and can read material well beyond grade level. He can retain much of what he hears and reads. He learns by self-involvement and by doing. While he is aware of his difficulty in writing, once he settles down, he tries to do his written work in spite of the obvious problem it presents for him.

He is realistically aware of his high reading level as well as his inability to produce legible written work.

Weaknesses

Bet has difficulty controlling his physical activity and often inadvertently disturbs those around him. He cannot organize his belongings or personal space such as his desk or locker.

Bet cannot structure or order his thinking when speaking and may ramble on and on.

He is highly distractible and may lose his train of thought or action by becoming involved in details along his way.

Bet tries to avoid all written work. His writing is messy, poorly formed, misspelled, and often illegible. His erasures often tear holes in his papers.

Socially, Bet does not perceive the needs or interests of others and cannot handle large, unstructured, free-play situations such as recess.

Behavior

Bet is continually active, often out of his seat. Even at work, Bet fidgets, although seated.

Bet disturbs those around him, sometimes unintentionally, sometimes just for something to do. Occasionally he finds himself in a scrap with another child who has "had it" and strikes back. Bet cannot understand why the other child is "picking on him."

Bet is unable to extend his concerns beyond himself to see the needs or interests of others and frequently misreads cues in a social situation.

Bet is highly frustrated by his inability to produce written work.

MODIFICATIONS IN EFFECT

1. Provide manipulative experiences where Bet can learn through doing and by his own discovery. Bet can learn better when working with his hands.
2. Provide thought structuring with beginning, middle, and end points. Help visualization by use of picture-cards or word-sequences.

3. Provide a frame for all output—artwork and written work. (*Example:* Writing paper with margins defined.)
4. Allow responses to be recorded on tape instead of written by hand.
5. Team Bet with a "secretary." Let Bet do the looking-up, have the secretary write the notes.
6. Simplify the social setting whenever possible. Have guided, structured activities during free-play periods.
7. Overlook Bet's physical activities while he is working, as long as he does not disturb others or disrupt the class. It is necessary for Bet to have an outlet for his physical energy even while he is concentrating.
8. Provide ways for Bet to alternate passive and active classtime. For example, help Bet put his energy to work. Allow him to pass out materials, get library books, etc.
9. Teach him to assist with audiovisual equipment.
10. Reduce demand for written work. Allow written, one-word answers instead of whole sentences; assign two instead of five questions.
11. Appreciate and praise his written effort for content and intent—de-emphasize spelling, structural flaws, and messy appearance.

Specific Skills Training*

Provide motor training to develop fine motor coordination.
Teach Bet to type. It will free him from the constraints of

---

*The training of specific skills is possible only in the secular school. Yet since this will eventually produce an effect on Bet's work and behavior in religious school, it is helpful for the religious school teacher to be aware of this program.

fine motor production and allow him to put more of his effort into thought and less into worry about how to produce each letter.

Provide perceptual-motor training to develop gross motor coordination, spatial orientation, and body-image awareness.

LEARNING STYLE

Bet learns best through material presented in writing and/or direct physical work with materials or units so that he can work out his own conclusions. Structure must be provided for him for thought, and verbal and written output. It is also helpful to demonstrate directions for Bet.

IMPLICATIONS FOR THE RELIGIOUS SCHOOL: THE TEACHER SPEAKS

This information from the parents and the school provides a perspective on Bet that I wouldn't be able to guess on my own. I've learned that he can't express himself in writing the way he can orally because he is unable to write at fifth-grade level. Now I understand that behind much of Bet's behavior is his frustration with his inability to communicate his ideas in writing. Added to this frustration is his awareness of the inconsistencies in his school work performance. He's so bright that this confuses him.

I understand through these reports how important it is to capitalize on Bet's strengths. I can provide alternatives to written assignments. Now I know Bet enjoys history so I can send him to the library to look up and read about famous

Jewish personalities in the specific areas we're studying. Bet can do Israel study for our research and orally present it to the class. He can read biographies of Ben-Gurion, Golda Meir, or Moshe Dayan and tell how they influenced modern Jewish history. If we're studying prophets, he can go directly to the Bible to see how these ancient visionaries shaped Jewish history. If it's life in Eastern Europe, then Bet can tell the class about Chasidism and our great-grandparents' way of life.

I can put Bet in a situation where he is teamed with another child who does well with written work. Because of his ability to read Bet can provide the information while his teammate puts the ideas on paper. I don't have to worry about the reading-material level because Bet now reads almost two years above his grade. Since he's eager to seek out and share information, Bet will be in demand by his classmates. However, if a lesson is planned to team up all the children, Bet won't stick out as "teacher's pet," a "bookworm," or "egghead."

History bees and games that allow for oral answers will give Bet the encouragement he needs to have a positive religious school experience. The tape recorder can be a valuable tool for Bet. He could take his exams by reading the questions and then recording his oral answers on tape.

We can follow the modifications given by the secular school just as well in religious school. Providing structure for written work and putting Bet's energy to work won't require extra effort on my part but can make an important difference in Bet's attitude.

I recognize that Bet can't sit still and I won't pressure him to. I'll accept his activity level provided he isn't annoying others.

CHILD GIMEL

Religious School Teacher Observations

This child is characterized by his passivity. Gimel never talks out of turn and his behavior is that of silence. He appears to be part of the class as the minimum class requirements are accomplished. However, since he never volunteers, the teacher cannot tell if he does or does not know the answers. Gimel answers when called upon but is not visibly bothered if his answer is incorrect. His answers are brief using only a few words. He follows directions and will do projects as required, but in a perfunctory manner. Because of the passive nature of Gimel, this problem may not manifest itself until report cards are being prepared and then the teacher realizes that Gimel deserves an *A* in conduct but an *F* in effort! The teacher feels this child could do better if he would only try harder.

Because of his silence in class Gimel is often overlooked and to some degree ignored by the teacher, while a more verbal child demands and may monopolize the teacher's attention. Gimel seems to have a wall between his physical and mental presence in class. He seems detached from the classroom situation. The teacher may wonder, "where is he?"

It seems that he has no friends in class since the other students do not talk to or socialize with him. They act as if he is not there and forget to include him in group projects.

Conversation with Parents

Gimel is a quiet child who works or plays alone or with a few friends who share his interest in games of strategy. His school grades are good. Gimel never seems to have to try hard and tends to take it for granted that he will do well with no effort. He reads science fiction novels at an adult level. Gimel is in religious school because his parents want him to be confirmed.

SCHOOL REPORT

Gimel does not have a learning disability. In fact, Gimel is a highly gifted child with a capacity for understanding that far exceeds his years. He presents a problem to the teacher who has to find materials stimulating enough to challenge him. Gimel has a tendency to tune out and turn off the classroom unless he is personally involved in preparing or participating in some special project.

Aware of his unique abilities, Gimel prefers to keep to himself and to purposely underachieve in relation to his abilities, rather than be set apart as different by his peers. He has not yet come to terms with how to live with his special gifts.

Likewise, his peers are uncertain about how to relate to him and therefore tend to leave him out.

IMPLICATIONS FOR THE RELIGIOUS SCHOOL: THE TEACHER SPEAKS

I wouldn't be able to pinpoint a specific learning problem or difficulty from my own observations of Gimel. But I question his resistance and lack of participation. After reading the school report and meeting with his parents, I learned much about Gimel and now I can use that knowledge to prepare lesson plans. Because he has such a great capacity for learning and problem-solving, Gimel can expand on the learning we do in class by reading adult-level history books and books dealing with interpretations of history. Because I know he likes games of strategy, I can have him chart the various strategies of the prophets in their quest for the Jewish people to carry out God's commandments. Perhaps he can map the battles of the Jewish people in ancient Canaan as well as in modern Israel. As history is a significant focus of Jewish learning all through the religious school years, it's possible to pull Gimel into the classroom situation if he feels it's worthwhile and challenging. Gimel can convert history into strategic planning and help put it into perspective for himself as well as for others. I can ask these kinds of strategy questions along with charts and maps to help Gimel use his strengths in classroom work: *How did the Hagana manage to outwit the British during the Palestinian Mandate? What were the steps leading to the final destruction of the Second Temple and the beginning of the long Diaspora?* He could strategically plan the exodus of the Israelites from Egypt and plot the battle of Jericho. Gimel could spend time piecing together our Jewish history. And, like Bet, it would be good to team him with others so that he will not feel left out. This would create an atmosphere where his knowledge would be sought by his peers.

It was important that I question Gimel's behavior. Otherwise I would never have known how to pull him into the classroom experience. But I also learned from Gimel that surface behaviors can be the same for two or three children but that the reasons behind these behaviors are different.

The "Gimel Question"

In this instance, Child Gimel is highly gifted. Gimel is a problem because he *will not* perform by choice, as opposed to the child who *cannot* perform due to a basic functional problem.

POSSIBLE ANSWERS

A. Gimel is challenging as his non-performance is a result of affect—motivational and emotional factors—and not of function. Gimel's problem is partly of his own choosing, with his abilities consciously withheld. We included Gimel because he exists in the classroom, and because he presents a particular kind of individual need.

B. A similar description could fit the observable classroom behavior of a child with a learning disability who cannot focus or sustain attention and who would require modification techniques in the classroom other than those which were previously described.

C. Another possibility for this overt behavior is the child with a low energy threshhold who is genuinely fatigued at the end of the secular school day. It must be recognized that for some children religious school comes when that child simply cannot handle a further workload. The teacher must then try to initiate strategies which draw the child personally into the sphere of the classroom action. This may mean making relatively simple classroom modifications such as seating the child near the teacher, or near ventilation; it may mean allowing a snack time at the beginning of class; it may mean asking the child to perform particular tasks that the child would not voluntarily do. It is clear that the ability is there—but the energy is not. Unless the teacher draws such a child out, ability will remain hidden.

It is critical for teachers to formulate questions and seek the answers for individual children. The subtleties involved in observing, questioning, and understanding require that one be a sensitive and insightful teacher.

CHILD DALET

RELIGIOUS SCHOOL TEACHER OBSERVATIONS

Dalet does very well with projects that physically involve him and he can work on them a long time to completion. However, he has difficulty in reading and is doing way below his fifth-grade level. He wants to get away from the academic areas of reading, papers, and worksheets. His successes are in creative areas of his own trial-and-error experimentation and not as a result of directions given by the teacher. He has his own criterion for success and he will persevere until he feels successful.

Dalet has difficulty distinguishing sounds, which affects both his Hebrew and English work and his ability to take directions. He cannot follow directions with more than two steps involved, such as "Please take out your Hebrew books and your notebooks and begin reading to yourselves on the top of page twelve. Page ten of your workbooks should be completed by the end of the period." Most children in fifth grade can handle such directions by this time. Dalet cannot.

Changes confuse Dalet especially if he is having success with some area of work and is feeling comfortable with it. For example, he ignores the directions that tell him it is time to put away a project and take out a book. He is reluctant to give up satisfying school work experiences and is unwilling to try the unknown. He does not want to risk failure and insists on remaining in a secure work setting. He will emphatically say "No, I'm not doing that, I'm doing this!"

Dalet works well in a group setting when he feels comfortable in it. He enjoys the other children as well. However, during an arts-and-crafts project he will remain by himself at his desk and does not acknowledge those around him if they should ask a question or want to chat or socialize. He becomes locked into his own work oblivious to what is going on around him. He appears to be a perfectionist in his work.

CONVERSATION WITH PARENTS

Dalet is pleasant and sociable and able to occupy himself for long periods of time. He enjoys creative projects of all kinds—the more complex the better. He works projects through without reading the directions—"you ought to see him when he is at work. It's almost as if he's in a world of his own!"

Dalet generally knows what it is he wants to do and sticks to it. It is hard to get him to change from one activity to another once he becomes involved in something.

Dalet seldom reads anything but simple comics. He prefers to do things in his own time in his own way. Dalet balks at being told *how* to do anything.

Dalet enjoys the company of other youngsters but is equally happy to pursue independent projects.

Parents are aware that Dalet is a bright youngster and offer to do whatever they can at home to help him achieve success in school.

SCHOOL REPORT
Grade: 5
Reading Level: Third grade
Writing Level: Third grade

Strengths
Dalet is of above-average intellect, testing in the superior range on the WISC-R Intelligence Test. He is capable of sustained purposeful activity particularly with creative or manipulative materials. He is able to work complex problems to solution through trial-and-error experimentation. He is sociable and gets along well with his peers. Dalet is capable of highly mature insight and provocative questioning when participating in group discussion.

Weaknesses
Dalet is well below grade level in reading and writing ability. Reversals and transpositions occur in both oral reading and writing. Dalet also has a tendency to slur his words thus producing indistinct speech.

He approaches his work in disorganized fashion. He is overwhelmed by complex speech or directions. He often proceeds on his own with no regard for directions, given either orally or in writing. Once involved in a successful activity, Dalet perseverates and resists change. He has difficulty in shifting activities and also in shifting from one physical environment to another.

His writing is fluent, but on an output level equal to his third-grade reading level. Occasional letters are reversed, although for the most part, letters are well-formed.

Dalet often exhibits confusion between right and left direction in writing and when involved in physical activity.

Behavior

Dalet gets along well with his peers. He can also work independently. When faced with potentially frustrating new activity, Dalet becomes insistent on remaining with the familiar
and successful rather than risk failure.

MODIFICATIONS IN EFFECT

1. Dalet works best when allowed to work problems
   through with three-dimensional manipulative
   materials.
2. For directed activity, he must work in successive small
   steps to completion. He must be given directions in
   simple, singular, step-by-step units. In this way he
   will combine small parts to achieve and understand a
   larger concept.
3. His creative approaches to problem solving are accepted and supported by the teacher.
4. When something must be done in just one way, a
   visual step-by-step model is provided.
5. Strengthen self-image by praising successes.
6. Pre-establish a *set* for each activity through a written
   time schedule, combined with verbal advance warning
   before activities will change. ("In five minutes we will
   be ready to clean up." "In ten minutes we will go to
   gym," or "At 3:30 we will have gym.")
7. Seat Dalet near teacher or speaker so he can focus on
   lip movements.
8. Minimize the need for written output in complex conceptual areas. Allow for tape-recorded answers for
   homework.

9. Accept and praise his output of third-grade level with the same support you would give to his peer producing fifth-grade work.
10. Provide reading materials at his level of capability.

SPECIFIC SKILLS TRAINING

Public school is providing a remediation program including speech therapy, and reading and writing tutorials on a one-to-one basis.

LEARNING STYLE

Dalet requires a readiness set for each activity. He needs simple discrete units of work or direction. He learns best by doing. Visual-tactile methods work most effectively for Dalet.

IMPLICATIONS FOR RELIGIOUS SCHOOL: THE TEACHER SPEAKS

I have a very good feeling after meeting with Dalet's parents because I know they're willing to help him regularly with his assignments and want religious school to be a positive experience. At the same time I'm aware that parents and children can work together in varying degrees. Also I don't know how well Dalet will accept his parents doing assignments with him. When parents offer to help with homework it should be on a trial-and-error basis with a way out built in—no long-range plans should be developed. It should be done one step at a time. If it proves successful, then it can be done again.

Because of Dalet's way of doing things—which may give a surface appearance of negativism—his behavior may be misinterpreted by others around him. If this proves to be the case with the parent, the conflict that may arise between parent and child puts the religious school in the middle. In other words, *parental willingness to help does not always insure success for the child, but it does keep the lines of communication open between religious school and home.*

The public school supplied information about Dalet which changed my whole attitude toward him. I now understand why I thought of him as stubborn when he was asked to shift from one activity to another but didn't. Now I know that he can't. The school made me aware that Dalet may become locked into an activity, particularly one with which he is experiencing success. A low self-image is so much a part of Dalet that he doesn't want to risk failure when confronted with unknown situations.

What I need to do in religious school is to put *steps for readiness* into my lesson plans—that is, structures and guidelines to help Dalet get ready for discussion if we're doing manual activity and vice versa. This will give him a readiness to shift gears by preparing him in advance for a change. I can do this in a variety of ways: by saying it, by writing it on the board, and by pointing to it as I read it. "At 3:30 we will begin cleaning up." At 3:30 I could say, "In five minutes we will begin our discussion on *The Story About the Twins at Camp Kee Tov.*" I can go over to him and see if he has responded. I'll follow the public school's suggestions when I give directions: provide as much visual input as possible and reinforce his self-image with praise. "You did a fine job following directions, Dalet." I won't expect fifth-grade written work from him and I can appreciate the thought behind his work while I deemphasize his writing skills and spelling.

Because of Dalet's considerable problem with reversals in writing, reading, and speech, it would appear that formalized learning of Hebrew at this time could only cause him one more failure for the school year. In his mind, his very Jewishness is at stake. This isn't a decision I can make alone, but it is an important area to be discussed together with the principal, the rabbi, and the child's parents.*

DISCUSSION

Now that the observations, discussion with parents, and secular school modifications have been taken into account by the religious school teacher, the teacher is better equipped to put a positive approach into future lessons. Now that students are understood as individuals in a total group, life in the classroom can be much more viable. All the complex information just given is not meant to intimidate or frighten the teacher in the religious school. This information is given to make lesson planning less demanding by understanding how classroom success may be accomplished through learning about individual differences.

To recapitulate: the teacher observed the children in the classroom setting and was puzzled as many questions formed about specific individuals. Being a good observer is the first step in finding solutions. Next, interacting with the parents and letting them know about specific concerns opens the door for communication between home and school, which is vital for the Jewish identity of the child.

---

*...and special educator, if one is available to the religious school.

There are, however, parents who are concerned only with the end results of religious school and not the means to the end. They may be indifferent to religious school because of their own attitudes and a lack of Jewish background, or they may not have resolved their own ambiguities about Judaism in general and religious school in particular. For these parents, their children's education is up to the religious school alone. These parents make it more difficult for their children but when their children are in the class, the teacher is responsible to them and not to the parents *during that time.* It is the teacher who must therefore try to create a Jewish learning environment with each child.

The most valuable pieces of information received from the secular school are the modifications suggested and the best learning style. For the most part these suggestions are well within reach of and can be directly implemented in the religious school classroom. If there are terms or jargon used in the reports which need clarification, the secular school will have to be contacted for explanation.

Two important factors should be kept in mind by the religious school teacher. First, *no two children are going to experience the lesson and classroom work in the same way or with the same degree of intensity. No classroom experience is going to be a 100 percent happening.* What is important is that each child receives some degree of Jewish learning each classroom period so that however slowly, the Jewish ideas learned in school remain with that child when school is over. And this can happen if each child feels some degree of success in the religious school.

Second, *the religious school is not responsible for the child's remediation in basic reading and writing skills. That is the job of the secular school.* This should ease any frustration a teacher may have because the role of religious school teacher is thus further defined. The religious school is responsible for bringing as much living Judaism into the classroom as possible. If each teacher is sensitized to the individual needs of students, then through experimentation and trial and error the lesson plans will become easier to implement. As the school year progresses, and as many problems are solved (or at least lessened), the teacher will be less frustrated and will certainly develop more and more self-confidence in meeting individual needs.

7

Complete Lesson Plan:
Part I

Chapter 7, Part I will be based upon the following biblical passage:

Genesis 18:16-33

16The men set out from there and looked down toward Sodom, Abraham walking with them to see them off. 17Now the Lord had said, "Shall I hide from Abraham what I am about to do, 18since Abraham is to become a great and populous nation and all the nations of the earth are to bless themselves by him? 19For I have singled him out, that he may instruct his children and his posterity to keep the way of the Lord by doing what is just and right, in order that the Lord may bring about for Abraham what He has promised him." 20Then the Lord said, "The outrage of Sodom and Gomorrah is so great, and their sin so grave! 21I will go down to see whether they have acted altogether according to the outcry that has come to Me; if not, I will know."

22The men went on from there to Sodom, while Abraham remained standing before the Lord. 23Abraham came forward and said, "Will You

sweep away the innocent along with the guilty?
₂₄What if there should be fifty innocent within the
city; will You then wipe out the place and not
forgive it for the sake of the innocent fifty who are
in it? ₂₅Far be it from You to do such a thing, to
bring death upon the innocent as well as the guilty,
so that innocent and guilty fare alike. Far be it
from You! Shall not the Judge of all the earth deal
justly?" ₂₆And the Lord answered, "If I find
within the city of Sodom fifty innocent ones, I will
forgive the whole place for their sake." ₂₇Abraham
spoke up, saying "Here I venture to speak to the
Lord, I who am but dust and ashes: ₂₈What if the
fifty innocent should lack five? Will You destroy
the whole city for want of the five?" And He
answered, "I will not destroy if I find forty-five
there." ₂₉But he spoke to Him again, and said,
"What if forty should be found there?" And He
answered, "I will not do it, for the sake of the forty." ₃₀And he said, "Let not the Lord be angry if I
go on: What if thirty should be found there?" And
He answered, "I will not do it if I find thirty
there." ₃₁And he said, "I venture again to speak to
the Lord: What if twenty should be found there?"
And He answered, "I will not destroy, for the sake
of the twenty." ₃₂And he said, "Let not the Lord
be angry if I speak but this last time: What if ten
should be found there?" And He answered, "I will
not destroy, for the sake of the ten." ₃₃When the
Lord had finished speaking to Abraham, He
departed; and Abraham returned to his place.*

The information from chapter 6 can now be used in actual
lesson planning; the modifications suggested can be built
directly into the everyday lessons of the religious school. The
following is a presentation of a single Bible story for such
teaching and is not a major classroom project which takes

The Torah: The Five Books of Moses. A new translation of *The Holy Scriptures*
according to the Masoretic Text, First Section © 1962.

several sessions to complete. The technique and modifications discussed in the analysis of this lesson can be used regularly in the religious school.

FIFTH-GRADE BIBLE LESSON = 1½ hours:
Abraham Questions God

Goals: 1. To teach students to look up a reference in the Bible.
2. To develop an understanding of why Abraham was a good choice to be the father of the Hebrew people (using the Sodom and Gomorrah story, Genesis 18:16-33).
3. To have students understand God's role in the dialogue (Genesis 18:16-33).

First half: Read Genesis 18:16-33 together as a class; follow by discussion on these questions:
1. What are God and Abraham doing?
2. What does Abraham think of God's plan?
3. Why does God answer Abraham as He does?
4. What is different about how God is talking with Abraham in this chapter compared to the way He talked to him before?

Second half: Divide the students into groups of three; within each group there are three functions to fill:
1. a reader
2. a secretary
3. a Bible illustrator

All in the individual group work together, each doing a specific job:

1. The reader rereads Genesis 18:16-33 aloud to the group (the other students follow the narration in their own books) and decides with the group what words describe Abraham and what words describe God. While the secretary and illustrator are doing their work, the reader silently reads another Abraham story, Genesis 22:1-13, to gain more insight into Abraham's character. The reader is also asked to think through the following: 1) how is God acting differently in the two stories? 2) how is Abraham acting differently? Later these ideas will be shared with the whole class.

2. The secretary rewrites the story as a dialogue between Abraham and God on mimeo paper so that it can be shared with the whole class as a news brief. This could also be decorated. (In some instances the secretary and illustrator may spontaneously interact.)

3. The illustrator depicts the scene as would a Bible illustrator. These pictures will go on the bulletin board.

Before the groups form to start their work, the teacher defines the duties of each group member and points out possible problems, such as how a Bible illustrator is able to draw a picture in which God is part of the story. Through class discussion and some ideas from the teacher, answers will emerge.

Most fifth graders are mature enough to handle many concepts about people and God which are portrayed in biblical stories. This particular discussion about how illustrations involving God are handled could include the question, Is God a person? In the Bible God is given characteristics of humans to help explain the morals, values, and conflicts of the personalities involved. A teacher could well anticipate a child bringing up the earlier biblical passage of human beings being created in the image of God. Then the teacher could point out that our Jewish tradition teaches us that we have the power within us to understand God through our good works toward others. In other words, the likeness of people to God is spiritual rather than physical. As Jews we do not limit God's abundant powers by something as concrete as a picture. What we *can do* is to illustrate God's wonders which manifest themselves everywhere in nature and in the good deeds of human beings. Some copies of Jewish manuscripts could be brought into class to show how artists in earlier generations handled the concept.

ANALYSIS OF THE ABOVE LESSON PLAN

First half: The page number for the Sodom and Gomorrah story (Genesis 18:16-33) is written on the board in advance. Pointing to the board, each item is then explained.

a. Genesis is the book
b. 18 is the chapter
c. 29 is the page number
d. the Hebrew for Genesis is

בְּרֵאשִׁית

Thus given 18:16-33--18 represents the chapter in Genesis, 16-33 represents the sentences to be read, and 16 begins about halfway through the chapter.

For reinforcement the teacher asks the students to find two other Bible sources such as 20:1-3 in Genesis and chapter 2:1-5 in Exodus.

A copy of the illustration should be available on a small poster so that individuals can see it at closer range. It should also be there for continued visual reference when the board is used for other material.

During the first half of the lesson some children may remain passive and not volunteer to read or participate in the class discussion of the questions following the reading. However, during the second half of the lesson each child will have more direct involvement and input.

When the class breaks to form groups during the second half of the lesson, it is advantageous for the teacher to assign students to each group. Teachers are often reluctant to do this because they think independent grouping provides the best group experience for students. However, a knowledge of pupil strengths and weaknesses may make teacher intervention essential. In this fifth-grade class it's possible that Gimel (our gifted but shy pupil) may not have been chosen to be part of a self-selected group. (In other classroom work such as music, dramatics, or art projects, self-grouping could be very effective.)

Once the groups are established, it is helpful for the teacher to also assign specific roles within each group. The power of suggestion may help each child fulfill the assigned role. For example, "Dalet (a poor reader), you'd make a fine illustrator for your group," or "Bet (an above-average reader), I'd like you to be the reader in your group."

It is very easy to fall into the trap of leaving too many options open to students and every teacher has done this. Look what could happen if the teacher said, "Alef, why don't you be the reader?" or "Wouldn't you like to be the reader, Alef?" These kinds of suggestions put the decision on the student and the response may well be, "No, I don't want to be the reader!" The lesson then begins with negative feelings.

By placing each student in a group and by giving each one a role, the teacher is assured that the group setting is suited to the individual needs of the students. The lesson begins on a positive note.

Once the groups are formed, the teacher reviews with each group the job that each member of that group is to do. A few key words written on the board by the teacher will reinforce the directions.

Example:

Reader	*Secretary*	*Illustrator*
1. Read Genesis 18:16-33 with the group	1. Read with the reader Genesis 18:16-33	1. Read with the reader Genesis 18:16-33
2. Decide what words describe God and Abraham	2. Help decide and write down what words describe God and Abraham	2. Help decide what words desribe God and Abraham
3. Read Genesis 22:1-13 and think about how God and Abraham act differently in each of the two stories	3. Rewrite the story on mimeo paper	3. Illustrate the Bible scene
4. Report to the teacher at	4. Report to the teacher at	4. Report to the teacher at

Each student reports to the teacher at the assigned time. This system helps the teacher to see everyone's progress and to give each student additional support—directly and personally. Further, it provides a specific time to ask questions.

A level of expectation or readiness for change can be built into the lesson itself to help insure a smooth transition in classroom activity. For example, if the class begins at 3:30 P.M., then at 4:45 P.M. the teacher says, "In five minutes we will clean up and get ready to go home. We will have time tomorrow to finish the work." At 4:50 P.M., "It's clean-up time. Prepare your books and papers to go home. Then get your coats." Even if the bell rings (as it often does while students are preparing to leave), it is important for the teacher to make a few brief closing remarks to the class. These may include:

1. Support for the accomplishments of the class.
2. A summary statement regarding the righteousness of Abraham and the example he set for us.
3. The schedule for the next session regarding the completion of the work. This will put into perspective what was done today and lead to anticipation of the next lesson.

In summary: during the first half of the lesson there was no pressure for anyone to read either aloud or silently. This was a relief for Alef. Also beneficial to Alef were the visual models present throughout the second half of the lesson, and the reinforcement of listening and looking at directions simultaneously. There was an additional reading assignment for Bet and Gimel which allowed them to analyze the two Bible stories.

There was no pressure put on Bet to write down his thoughts. And so important for Dalet, the time expectation and readiness factor was built into this lesson.

It should also be noted that because of the limited written output required in this lesson for Bet and Dalet, the teacher made only one modification yet helped both children at the same time.

As a teacher, therefore, it is possible to cut down on time in preparing lessons because one modification often meets contrasting needs. For Bet who writes at third-grade level but who conceptualizes questions and directions well, this lesson capitalized on his understanding of the ideas presented in the Bible stories. It minimized his weakness. For Dalet who had difficulty conceptualizing ideas and who physically cannot handle the demands of written work, his assignment to illustrate rather than write eliminated a potentially stressful situation. Instead he was given an opportunity to explore manipulative art materials which provided for a more satisfying experience.

The grouping allowed all the children in the class to capitalize on their interests and to share ideas. While the modifications used were a must for specific individuals, they were also of great value to the entire class. Alef, Bet, and Dalet could not be put within the same group but were joined with other members of the class. Gimel could be grouped with any of the children including Alef, Bet, and Dalet. The preparation of a structured time chart was not a burden to the teacher and its presence in fact helped the entire classroom period to run more smoothly. This was only one lesson plan. The variations of this plan—and the countless other lessons within the religious school year are limitless.

Follow-Up Lesson:
Part II

BY NOW YOU ARE WELL ACQUAINTED WITH THE FOUR STUDENTS Alef, Bet, Gimel, and Dalet. They are profiled in the chart appearing on pp. 118 and 119. In this profile the teacher can easily see areas of strength for individual students as well as areas where one modification may suit the needs of more than one child. The chart is designed to be used with flexibility in order to provide the teacher with a summary of important information of special needs students.

As you read this follow-up lesson, it may be possible, using the information you have about these children, for you to think of materials and activities other than those indicated in the follow-up lesson which is developed in this chapter.

The follow-up lesson will include the following biblical passage:

Genesis 22:1-13

₁Some time afterward, God put Abraham to the test. He said to him, "Abraham," and he answered, "Here I am." ₂And He said, "Take your son, your favored one, Isaac, whom you love, and go to the land of Moriah, and offer him there as a burnt offering on one of the heights which I will point out to you." ₃So early next morning, Abraham saddled his ass and took with him two of

116

his servants and his son Isaac. He split the wood for the burnt offering, and he set out for the place of which God had told him. ₄On the third day Abraham looked up and saw the place from afar. ₅Then Abraham said to his servants, "You stay here with the ass. The boy and I will go up there; we will worship and we will return to you."

₆Abraham took the wood for the burnt offering and put it on his son Isaac. He himself took the firestone and the knife; and the two walked off together. ₇Then Isaac said to his father Abraham, "Father!" And he answered, "Yes, my son." And he said, "Here are the firestone and the wood; but where is the sheep for the burnt offering?" ₈And Abraham said, "God will see to the sheep for His burnt offering, my son." And the two of them walked on together.

₉They arrived at the place of which God had told him. Abraham built an altar there; he laid out the wood; he bound his son Isaac; he laid him on the altar, on top of the wood. ₁₀And Abraham picked up the knife to slay his son. ₁₁Then an angel of the Lord called to him from heaven: "Abraham! Abraham!" And he answered, "Here I am." ₁₂And he said, "Do not raise your hand against the boy, or do anything to him. For now I know that you fear God, since you have not withheld your son, your favored one, from Me." ₁₃When Abraham looked up, his eye fell upon a ram, caught in the thicket by its horns. So Abraham went and took the ram and offered it up as a burnt offering in place of his son.*

The Torah: The Five Books of Moses. A new translation of *The Holy Scriptures* according to the Masoretic Text, First Section © 1962.

ALEF	BET
Mid-Third Grade	**High Sixth Grade**
Mid-Third Grade	Third Grade
• good auditory memory for information in context • good in music (songs) • good in creative art • long attention span for creative activities • high (5th grade) conceptual level	• very bright, alert, and curious • seeks challenging books to read independently (history) • good retention of written material • learns by doing • self-motivated • aware of personal strengths and weaknesses
• reading comprehension • difficulty in following directions • poor retention of spoken information • difficulty in beginning oral answers	• disorganized, distractible, overactive (may bother others unintentionally) • messy, unreadable papers (avoids writing) • problems in relating to classmates, especially in unstructured situations • frustrated by own poor written work
• give short, simple directions • provide visual models • allow private time with teacher each session • encourage participation in discussions, provide starting points or verbal cues • give tests orally • give extra signs of approval • provide creative art and music experiences • shorten assignments, both reading and writing	• assign research • team with secretary • use tape recorder • give tests orally • structure thought: start-finish • structure written work • shorten assignments • praise own written work • tolerate hyperactivity, within limits • provide opportunities for learning-by-doing • involve in physical activity
• learns best when material is presented aloud and in context, and when accompanied by visual or action reinforcement	• learns best when in direct contact with material • works out own conclusion • needs structure for thought, verbal and written output • needs directions demonstrated • needs information presented in writing

CATEGORY	GIMEL	DALET
READING LEVEL	Gifted	Third Grade
WRITING LEVEL	Gifted	Third Grade
STRENGTHS	• exceptionally bright; interested in science fiction, games of strategy	• high intellect; can work out solutions to problems by experimentation • can stay with an activity until completion • sociable with peers • adds insight to class discussion
WEAKNESSES	• purposefully underachieves • tunes out classroom • overlooked by peers	• reversals in oral reading and writing • indistinct speech • work is disorganized • overwhelmed by complex directions and disregards them • resists change • exhibits directionality confusions
MODIFICATIONS	• provide challenging books • assign historical strategies to plot out • involve in team projects in which classmates will respect abilities	• present work in small steps • provide work in 3-dimensional material • provide visual model • praise successes • provide time schedule (both written and oral) • seat near teacher • provide reading material at third-grade level
LEARNING STYLE		• requires readiness set for each new activity • needs simple units of work or directions • learns by doing • learns by visual-tactile methods

The follow-up lesson will include the biblical passage of Genesis 22:1-13 as well as the biblical passage of Genesis 18:16-33 already studied in the preceding lesson. This lesson will have two parts to it. Part I will be devoted to the completion of the work begun during the first lesson and also the reading of Genesis 22:1-13. Part II will be a review section in which the messages of the two biblical passages will be brought together.

PART I

1. The secretaries complete their stories and write them on Ditto paper to be run off.
2. The illustrators complete their pictures on poster board and place them on the bulletin board.
3. The readers meet with the teacher to discuss the differences that they found between the two Bible stories (Genesis 18:16-33 and Genesis 22:1-13) concerning the behaviors of Abraham and God.

(This section of the lesson, with its built-in flexibility, should meet the needs of the individual students. Therefore, it may be beneficial to stop at this point to evaluate what is happening in the classroom:

Three different activities are going on at the same time.
Three groups of children are working in their best learning style.
Specifically, the readers with their greater reading fluency were given the opportunity to explore the ideas presented in Genesis 22:1-13.)

When the above three steps are completed, the students again convene as one group and, with volunteers reading aloud, follow the text of the second biblical passage (Genesis

22:1-13). The teacher then leads a discussion focusing on these questions:
   a. How did Abraham and God speak to each other in both biblical stories?
   b. What do these conversations tell us about Abraham? about God?

The class is now ready to move into the second part of the follow-up lesson which reviews the two biblical stories in an entirely different manner as a complement to the earlier presentation. Note that the closing remarks built in an anticipatory set for the follow-up lesson and facilitated a quick and smooth transition. This simple modification required no extra work by the teacher, yet greatly helped particular students to be ready for the next class session.

PART II

For a review in which the above Bible stories will be included, a different approach should be used from that used in the first lesson. In the first lesson, certain modifications were used to meet some specific needs of the individuals in the class. In the review section of the follow-up lesson, other modifications will be used to meet *other* needs of these same individuals. In this way the teacher avoids getting into a rut by *not* doing the same kind of activity with the same children.

To begin with, students receive copies of the Dittos prepared earlier by the secretaries. These provide continuity and introduction to the review lesson. Then, in the review described below, methods are used which avoid the more usual paper-and-pencil tasks that students perform in so much of their secular and religious education.

Charts and games requiring motor and tactile experimentation and manipulative materials requiring action and learning-by-doing meet many needs for the child with a learning disability. Here are some suggestions to be implemented in the second part of the follow-up lesson.

ORGANIZATION CHART*

Attach four pockets to a large colored poster board using a different color for each pocket. The pockets can be made from any number of materials— paper, a scrap of wall-paper, a library pocket card.**

When lettering use a dark but not bright color. Some high shades of red, yellow, or fluorescent colors cause visual stress for some children.

Write sayings from each of the two stories on individual pieces of poster board or index cards. Place these in a large envelope or shoe box.

Students then go to the box and pick one of the sayings and place it into the proper pocket on the chart. Oatmeal boxes or

---

*Genesis 18:16-33 will be referred to as the Sodom and Gomorrah story.
Genesis 22:1-13 will be referred to as the Akedah story.
**Dolores Kohl. Jewish Teacher Center, Wilmette, Illinois.

egg cartons can be used in place of a chart—anything in which a card can be placed is acceptable. The organization chart or small boxes or envelopes can be used on a smaller scale at a child's desk for one or two students to use at a time.

Another review suggestion is the sequencing of events. The teacher writes the individual events in the Bible stories on poster boards that are small enough to hold by hand. The teacher gives each card to a child. The children stand at the front of the class and another student places the children so that the cards they are holding appear in the correct order. This can be done with pictures of the events instead of just words. On a smaller scale, as an individual activity, the sequencing can take place at the child's desk. If to be done by one child, the cards should be numbered on the back in proper sequence. This allows for self-checking. The teacher or teacher's aide can make one set, to be used by one child as a separate activity; or several sets can be made, using Ditto or Xerox, if this activity is planned for group use.

Another self-checking learning device is the "fact-flip." The teacher compiles a booklet of questions on cards, one question per card. Written on the bottom of each card are several possible answers, but only one is correct. Behind the

Dot appears on back of card
behind Isaac's name.

correct answer is a large colored dot and the child can check the answer by flipping the card over. The cards are held together with a ring.

For this lesson (as well as at other times during the year), vary the classroom environment by turning several different areas of the room into learning centers.* Each of the above visual aids and variations of them and other supplementary reading or creative activities should be placed around the room.

A few students at a time begin at each area and then rotate from one self-contained activity to another. Organization of time and selection of activities can be pre-planned by the teacher, taking into consideration the working dynamics of the class as a whole and of individuals in particular.

Each teacher brings a unique personality into the classroom, therefore the kinds of materials created for that classroom will vary greatly. Although the preceding suggestions represent only the beginning of creative planning, teachers can recognize a fresh and stimulating approach to learning in the religious school. More essentially students with specific problems were helped. Bet benefited because he wasn't required to sit still or to write. Alef was helped because she had self-checking available and built into some of the activities to give her immediate support. Dalet was helped through the use of visual and tactile materials and their manipulation. Gimel, as well as the rest of the class, benefited from the personal-involvement level built into the structure of the review used in the second part of this lesson.

---

*Discussion of learning centers appears in the magazine *Alternatives in Religious Education*, Winter 1977.

8

Setting the Tone of the Classroom

THE DYNAMICS OF A CLASSROOM ARE MULTIFACETED. BUT THE
teacher is the force behind it all. It is the teacher who sets the
tone. *Setting the tone is creating a mood or feeling which surrounds the students upon entering the classroom.* It includes
both the physical setting within the room and the emotional
climate between teacher and student, between student and
student, and perhaps, most importantly, the feeling the
students carry inside themselves when coming to or when
leaving the religious school. Everything is influenced by the
teacher's attitude, ability to communicate with students, skill
in organizing and structuring the time and space in which the
students are involved. These are critical factors for those
children who experience learning problems. Their educational problems can become less of a concern to them if their
primary association with religious school is one of positive
identity, a feeling of acceptance and belonging, and a feeling
of involvement with things Jewish.

Often teachers become preoccupied with lesson plans,
teaching religious observances and other specific Jewish
educational goals, and overlook the subtle, yet pervasive, effects involving the organization of the students' time and
space within the classroom.

As these factors are often taken for granted, this is an area
where assumptions are often made and important elements

may therefore be inadvertently overlooked. A closer look...and something doesn't fit or something is missing. The best planned lesson can fail if it takes place against a background where materials are missing, seating is inadequate, or where there is poor communication between teacher and student.

The following suggestions and explanations concerning classroom management and communication are offered here to be used with all children in the religious school, but with specific emphasis on those children with learning problems which require additional attention.

ORGANIZATION OF SPACE

1. *Seating Plan*

The physical aspects of the room help to create the mood. The room is often the first encounter a child has with the religious school. Will the child feel comfortable here? One way to help bring about this feeling of comfort and security is to arrange the chairs and desks in a predictable order and to keep this routine for some length of time. Should there be a need for classroom rearrangement during the year, the students will need preparation that a change is coming. Although the chairs will often be temporarily moved during projects and other classroom work, they should be returned to their original floorplan before class is over. It is important whatever the arrangement, to space seats so that they don't touch each other.

Many children with learning problems need known boundaries and limits in addition to the enclosure of a room. They need to know they have their own place within the four walls. In the elementary grades it is best for the teacher to assign the seat once the teacher becomes familiar with the individuals in the class.*

2. *Furniture*

The furniture itself is another element of the physical setting of the classroom. A child with a specific disability in directional awareness would have a problem with certain desk/chair designs. The desk with the large armrest covering part of the right side of the body (tablet chair) is familiar furniture in many religious schools but is the cause of much frustration to students. The whole body needs to turn to work at this kind of desk and there is no freedom of movement. The lack of space at this desk causes books, pencils, and papers to drop continuously. This can be a problem to all students. Left-handed children are doubly inconvenienced, and students already troubled with problems in organization will find themselves in a difficult work situation.

If available, a more suitable work area is a chair and long table, or a desk with a tabletop which covers the whole front of the body and which has a shelf underneath for books.

3. *Multi-Purpose Rooms*

In many religious schools, classrooms have multiple purposes and what is a classroom now may have been a meeting room the hour before, with ashtrays still on the desks. Or the room may serve more than one or two classes so that board space and display areas are shared and therefore limited. The desks may be arranged differently from the last class session, materials that were used previously and set aside for next time

---

*For junior-high students, social pressure and adolescent behavior are such that assigned seating could cause rebellion and a student could say, "I'm not going to religious school if I have to sit next to so-and-so." Trial-and-error seating and flexibility are even more necessary at this age level.

may have been moved or disturbed by another teacher or student. Nevertheless, if classes are to run smoothly, time must be spent with students instead of rearranging materials.

ORGANIZATION OF TIME

1. *Orientation Routines*

The routine within the classroom and a predictable series of events occurring in the classroom are important factors for children with learning disabilities who need sequential guidelines. Therefore, an order which can be followed and expected will meet these needs.

These routines can include, in order:

A. *Action attendance-taking. Some suggestions are:*
   a. Students take name tags in the shape of Jewish stars, dreidels, hamantashen, shofars, etc., from a bulletin board and transfer them to a large seating chart.
   b. Students sign in on the blackboard.
   c. With clothespins, students clip name tags in the shape of Jewish symbols (as in a.) to an attendance line that is always hung in one location. Younger children especially enjoy the variety of tags (which also introduces them to Jewish symbols).

B. *Hanging their outdoor clothing in an assigned location.* These areas can be decorated with the children's individual insignias taken from the twelve tribes or other Jewish symbols (such as a Torah mantle or Havdalah candle).

C. *Going to a learning center within the room.* This can be one designated area where Jewish educational games and materials are available for experimentation and thinking. These routines provide a means for action and involvement within a structured setting. Known limits are essential to many children with learning problems—the worry of "what do I do next?" is largely eliminated and the child is freed to experiment and to learn.

2. *Food for Thought*

Another element of the routine is to provide a snack shortly after beginning the session. This serves several purposes. First, the time spent having a snack enables students who may not see each other in secular school to socialize. In communities where the Jewish population is small, the religious school may be the only place where Jewish students get together. The religious school should encourage this concept and snack time is a good time to reinforce it.

Second, snack time gives the children a time to unwind and to make the transition from secular school to religious school. Third, it provides a feeling of warmth between the child and religious school and a feeling that one can relax a bit before new demands are made.

3. *Teacher Availability*

Another important part of the routine is the presence of the teacher when the child first arrives. Revealing conversations and feelings often are shared with the teacher before class begins.

Variations within routines can be handled smoothly if the standard routines are set first.

4. *Homework*

> I'm *not* going to write down the assignment for this child every week. A fifth grader is capable of writing down his own homework assignment!
>
> *Quote from a religious school teacher*

This angry statement was made to the principal when it was suggested that the teacher write down assignments for a particular student. The meeting between the teacher and the principal took place after the parents telephoned to find out why their child was having so much difficulty with the assignments. The fact is that there are some students who cannot write down their own assignments; there are some who cannot remember the assignment; there are some who cannot understand the assignment, and there are some who cannot do the assignment. No matter what the students' capabilities are, when they arrive home they may forget or not understand what their homework is or find they "didn't have time" to write down the assignment from the verbal explanation.

Some basic suggestions:

A. Make no assumptions.

B. Write assignments on the board for the class to copy using simple language. Write directions one step at a time. Help those who have difficulty copying, or simply give a particular student a copy of the directions to take home.

C. When the routine of classwork for the week can be anticipated, it may be an easy addition to prepare a Ditto sheet of assignments each week for all students to take home.

Ask the parents at the beginning of the school year to cooperate by going over the weekly assignment sheets with their children. Parents are helped also when they are familiar with the routines. This will give parents the opportunity to know what material is being covered in class and will serve as a backup when questions arise either from parents or students.

COMMUNICATION

1. *Behavior Problems*

Some basic discipline problems can be avoided if children know what is expected of them. Many acting-out behaviors are signs that certain children need order, particularly among those with specific behavior or learning problems.

Disruptive or immature behavior of any kind by some children causes others to have negative feelings about religious school. Individual classmates may say to the teacher, "He's disgusting, why don't you throw him out?" "Call the principal, she ruins it for the rest of us." In some instances, strong resentment is focused upon the individuals responsible for continuing disruption.

What can be done to alleviate this problem? Sometimes the simplest and easiest idea works best. Set aside a time to speak privately with the child before or after class, to discuss the problem. Some ideas on what might be talked about during this time are:

A. Let the child know that as a teacher you are concerned and want to help.

B. Encourage the child to discuss the feelings that arise when the class responds negatively to the disruptive behavior.

C. Help the child discuss the classroom atmosphere or activity at the time the trouble occurred.

D. Find out what interests the child. Does the child have a particular interest or strength that can be addressed in the religious school setting?

Who are the children causing and instigating undesirable behavior? They may be:

A. angry with parents who are forcing them to attend religious school.

B. those who could be involved with other afternoon or weekend activities such as scouts or sports.

    C. those who are rebellious against any authority and those who feel religious school "doesn't count."

    D. emotionally immature youngsters who need constant attention.

    E. youngsters who feel that they don't fit in with the rest of the group for some reason or another. Among these may be those with learning problems who already feel "different" during secular school and who act out during religious school.

Except for those children with specific school problems, a discussion with the child may be all that is needed. Or the parents, principal, and teacher may need to meet together with the child to show that the religious school means business and is a legitimate institution concerned with both the welfare of its students and the maintenance of its behavioral standards. For the child who feels out of place and acts out, the teacher and principal have to be particularly sensitive and observant so that workable solutions can be found. Here again trial-and-error experimentation by the adults is often the answer in helping the child.

2. *The Coat Syndrome*

The Coat Syndrome is a situation found in almost every religious school. Walk down any hallway in any religious school, peek into the rooms, and you will see children with their coats still on in the middle of the session. This behavior causes battles between teachers and students. What are these children telling us? For some, this may be defiance: "Let me out of here!" or "I'm going home soon!" or "I'd rather be somewhere else!" For others, the coat represents home and a security blanket: "I'm not comfortable here," or "I don't belong here," or "I don't want to be here." The routine of hanging up coats may solve some of this, but a better tone in the classroom is more helpful in creating a positive attitude toward religious school.

3. *Emotional Tone*

A. The classroom must show the students' work as soon as possible after the year begins. The work may be papers or projects or tapes recorded by students, or their thoughts and ideas written out by either the teacher or student hung on a bulletin board for all to see. *When a child sees that personal work is valued—and visible—part of that child remains in the room and reentering that room becomes a comfortable experience.* A child with a learning disability is most likely feeling unworthy during much of the long school day. The religious school needs to deal with this just as the essence of Judaism deals with each person as a valuable being, both singly and in relation to others. Each teacher has to work out how best to do this and to make creative materials available so that this process continues throughout the year. One of the most effective ways to use student work and to make it *visibly available* is to have students make their own creative teaching aids. When enough materials are available, they can be added to a learning center within the room and used by other students. This is one way in which the religious school will hold greater meaning for its students.

B. What is in the classroom that gives it its Jewish identity? And what sets it apart from secular school? These are questions to think about periodically during the school year. The teacher and students can work this out together to add to the Jewish-feeling tone in the classroom.

C. Another factor to consider when creating a good-feeling tone is regulating noise levels. For some children—and for some teachers as well—loud noise means confusion or causes confusion.

Some suggestions to help regulate noise levels within the classroom:

a. The teacher begins by example—speaking distinctly and never shouting above students' voices.

b. The teacher may use various exercises—facing away from the students and repeating a sentence in a whisper at first and then gradually speaking louder. After each repetition, ask students if they heard the sentence.

Do the same exercise of whispering a sentence and repeating it louder while facing the students. They'll discover that people can be understood by using speaking voices and not by shouting.

c. Have a *chalil* (Israeli flute) or bell in class. When the noise gets too loud play the instrument or ring the bell to signal that particular voices or the general noise level need lowering.

4.   *Giving Directions and Explanations*

Basically, a teacher communicates with students through the day-to-day giving of directions and explanations. One key to success in the classroom is the way in which the teacher presents the lesson, and often the best way is through multi-sensory methods.

Speaking, the common way to explain material to another person, requires articulate presentation and a responsive auditory recipient. However, tremendous concentration is required. At the end of the day many students coming to religious school simply do not have the ability to listen attentively. Children having difficulty with auditory processing will be tuned out altogether if lecturing or speaking is the only teaching method.

Explanations and directions are most effective when accompanied by an illustration. The illustration can be on the chalkboard as well as on a poster board that can be moved around for better visibility. *For example:* The subject is the Jewish National Fund and its role in the reclaiming of the land of Israel. Many words are needed to explain the hard work and progress of the *chalutzim.* When the teacher explains the barren land and swamps, pictures illustrating the concepts of barren and swampy may be shown to the children. The explanation is aided by visual examples. Often we assume certain words and terms are understood when in fact they are not.

It may be necessary to emphasize the main points of a text or to clarify a sequence of dates or events. The teacher can then write simple phrases about the important facts on poster board, using a separate board for each fact. Red, blue, or green lettering stands out better and is different from the print of the text. Then, as the teacher explains these facts, the poster boards can be held up in front of the students. Many children will learn a series of historical events if they can manipulate cards with events listed separately. For example, as a classroom activity: Have the students rearrange a set of chronological facts and put them in correct sequential order on the ledge of the blackboard or on a clothesline.

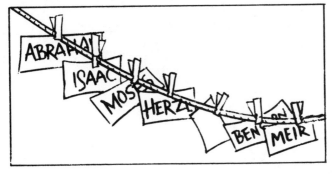

For individual activity at the children's desks, the teacher can show the students how to list facts or events on index cards. In this way the index cards can be manipulated by the children—placed on the floor for rearrangement, or shuffled and put into piles on the desk.

Projects which require many steps and that use a variety of materials need more than verbal explanations. The students need to go through the workings of the project, step by step, with a model already prepared by the teacher. In this way the children can see the project as it emerges from separate materials to finished product. Also the model provides a chance for the children to handle the materials to *see how they work.*

Children having difficulty in concentration and difficulty with processing of verbal material will need help with even the simplest directions ("Turn to page 31 in *Behold the Land*"). A large poster board prepared at the beginning of the year, with a picture of the book and the title and page number on top can be used throughout the school year changing only the page number as required. A paper clip can be used to clip on a card with each new assignment. The poster can be referred to as the teacher says "turn to page 31."

5. *Music Instruction*

When teaching Hebrew songs, whether in Hebrew or in transliteration, examine the formation and clarity of the letters—they may be inconsistent. This can be very confusing. The letters should look the same for each song and within the same song. Also the song may be visually divided into sections for easier learning. It can be helpful to some students if the leader uses a larger model of the song sheet or an opaque projector. Even with these aids, however, the words must be pointed to—one section at a time. Some children can pick up a song and learn it right away. But for others the song needs to be broken down both visually and auditorially into easily repeated sections. In some songs, perhaps only one word at a time can be learned, especially if that word has several syllables accompanied by several notes.

Music is an important part of our Jewish culture and variety in the technique of teaching music should be encouraged. For example, in the song "David Melech Israel," the song leader or assistant can hold up a picture of a king and a map of Israel every time those words are sung. These do not have to be elaborate and time-consuming pictures, just simple cues for the students. Soon the words can be eliminated altogether as the picture stimulates the correct response in the song. The children can beat the rhythm of the songs with simple instruments like bean shakers and paper horns brought from home or made in class.

6. *Self-Check Feedback*

How can educators best communicate with students? One suggestion is for the teacher to tape classroom sessions periodically during the school year. This may be one of the best ways to self-teach and to better understand how teachers appear to students.

These are the points to check while listening:

A. Is speech too fast?
B. Are words too complex for the grade level?
C. Are students being talked down to?
D. Is speech tone pitched for easy listening?
E. Does voice tone reflect acceptance or hostility? self-confidence or uncertainty or anxiety?
F. Is the teacher talking too much and not allowing enough time for student expression?

Summary

We have discussed many of the intricacies in setting the physical and emotional tone in the classroom. The goal in each area is to help students have a better feeling about themselves and their religious school experience. Often through a few simple modifications the religious school classroom can become a more comfortable and worthwhile place for all children.

The religious school teacher, working with children with learning disabilities, must develop a heightened awareness of the importance of structuring time and space within the classroom. Although most children need structure and organization to feel secure in the classroom, the learning disabled child can become overwhelmed and lost if there is a loose structure or no structure at all. There must be known and dependable parameters of these subtle yet often neglected elements of classroom management.

9

Hebrew: Some Classroom Strategies

MANY GOOD BOOKS HAVE BEEN WRITTEN ABOUT THE TEACHING of Hebrew. In this chapter, however, we are concerned with those methods which will benefit students with learning problems.

The Hebrew language is our link with past generations, with the people of Israel, and with our kindred Jews around the world. However, it can be a great frustration to beginning students. First, the letters are read and written from right to left which for many students is much in conflict with their English learning; second, the symbol code is entirely different from English letters; third, there are sounds which exist in Hebrew that do not exist in English, and fourth, Hebrew script does not correspond to the printed Hebrew text. For all students, whether they are adults or children, these differences require quite an adjustment. For the child with a severe learning disability who still has difficulty with English and who is being tutored in secular school, the learning of Hebrew could be a devastating experience.

For example, consider the multiple conflicts in the following progression and then try to imagine that you are a third-grade youngster beginning to learn the Hebrew language:

First you learn that in English the letter *s* produces
the sound heard at the beginning of the word *sit*.

Later you learn to associate that same sound heard at the beginning of *sit* with another letter—the letter *c* as in *cent*. There is now one sound associated with two different visual symbols. Add to this the *z* sound of the letter *s* that is heard in the word *busy*, and the *k* sound of the letter *c* that is heard in the word *cat*. You are thus faced with several choices for sounds that are associated with the visual letters *c* and *s*.

These complexities grow when two or more words look different and have different meanings but sound alike as in *sent, cent,* and even *scent.* And this is only in your English studies.

When you are in religious school you find that similar conflicts exist in Hebrew. Here too there can be two different letters for the same sound. For example, the *s* sound applies to the שׁ and ס as in the words שָׂמֵחַ and סָבָה . The *k* sound applies to both ק and כ as in the words קיר and כַּד .

But watch out! The dot on the *sin* can move to the other side of the letter to become a *shin* and represent the sound you heard at the beginning of *shalom.* Now you have to recognize a symbol and watch for moving dots as well.

Then there are letters that almost sound alike but that you still can't pronounce without choking or scratching your throat כ/ח/ך .

And of course there are the vowels and dots which almost seem to jump around the page. You find that a tiny dot can change a letter into something entirely different such as :

פ/פ   שׂ/שׁ   כ/כ   ב/ב

What? Now you have to learn to write script in Hebrew too? You find that the *shin* you knew as שׁ now is written Ϲ bearing no resemblance to what you have become familiar with in print. So a whole new visual set of symbolic representations must now be learned.

You further find yourself with strange-looking paper, fumbling as you work to write in the exact opposite direction from the way you are accustomed to writing English. *You don't need a learning problem to be confused at this point.* But, if you do have a learning problem, your difficulties and frustrations can be overwhelming indeed!

It may be that certain children cannot learn Hebrew at all if this conflict of languages represents a new and potentially severe source of frustration on top of the already existing problems in coping with their primary language of English. In many other cases the children will have to be tutored privately or taught with different techniques than those used in the classroom.

The magnitude of any decision to delay or to not teach Hebrew to a child must not be taken lightly. Many minor modifications are often possible and only in some instances is this major step taken. A learning disability specialist, either on the staff of or as a consultant to the religious school, can be invaluable in such vital decision-making.

The remainder of this chapter deals with a variety of techniques that can be used for all students who are beginning their Hebrew training. These techniques can be helpful to all students whether they are slow learners or quick learners. But for the children who have specific learning disabilities in acquiring language skills, the following suggestions and guidelines are useful additions to regular classroom techniques. By incorporating these strategies, it may be possible for children to enjoy and achieve success with the Hebrew language.

DIRECTIONAL AWARENESS

Before even the first letter of Hebrew is introduced, time should be spent on directional awareness. Do all students in the class know the difference between right and left? And is their own body awareness strong and secure?

Example: At the end of second grade a teacher was preparing the students for the next year and showing them how Hebrew is written from right to left using the word שָׁלוֹם . One little girl said to the teacher, "But I do it this way!" and proceeded to write on the board from left to right.

$$\text{שָׁ ל וֹ ם}$$
$$\text{1 2 3 4}$$

That little girl was secure with the knowledge of how things should be done on the basis of her experience with English. Now she had to learn a whole new—and conflicting—system of reading and writing.

Some suggestions for helping students understand the directional difference of Hebrew:

After explaining to the children* that Hebrew is the opposite of English in that it is read and written from right to

---

*Third-grade level, about eight years old, is the average time children begin their formal Hebrew training.

left, do some exercises and games with them. At first they may think it's silly, but as they become involved they'll think it's fun. *For example*, play *Shimon Omer* (Simon Says), demonstrating the required action:

a. hold your right *yad* (hand) up high
b. hold your right *yad* (hand) down low
c. kick your left *regel* (leg)
d. kick your right *regel* (leg)
e. touch your right *yad* (hand) to your left *berech* (knee)
f. touch your left *yad* (hand) to your right *berech* (knee)
g. walk to the right side of the *cheder* (room)
h. jump to the left side of the *cheder* (room)
i. put your left elbow up in the *avir* (air)
j. pick up your *iparon* (pencil) with your left hand

Once the children are secure with the nouns of *yad, regel,* and *cheder*, etc., play the game again and add the directional words of *yamin* and *semol* (right and left).
Example: "Hold your *yad yamin* high"; "Hold your *yad semol* down."

When the children learn these, add the verbs. Eventually the entire game can be played using mostly Hebrew. While initially at the beginning of the school year the purpose of the game is to reinforce the concepts of right and left, a later development becomes the utilization of Hebrew language.

Practice opening the Hebrew textbooks from right to left as well as doing the body exercises. In the beginning almost all students will have trouble remembering the directional differences. Some children will need help throughout the entire first year.

If at all possible, the teacher should prepare the Hebrew notebook paper with cues like this:

red letters   green letters

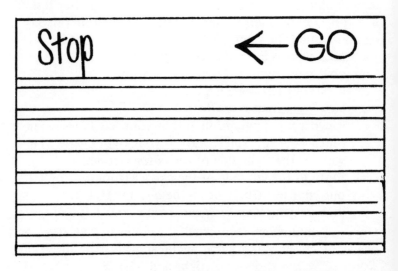

This will be a great help for all children just beginning to learn Hebrew, but it will aid specifically those students who consistently need a starting point. The standard Hebrew notebooks alternate small spaces and large spaces. It makes more sense to prepare Ditto sheets with large spaces until the children are at ease with Hebrew letter formation.

To help the children focus on the direction of writing, wear a colored streamer of crepe paper around the wrist when demonstrating at the board. In addition, as the teacher demonstrates the letters on the board, oral input that draws attention to the direction of the hand will help students to better remember. *For example*, with the letter *mem* say א "down-up-down." For the letter *lamed* say ל "down-across-down."

Some children who are left-handed and have trouble writing in English may have an easier time writing in Hebrew. When writing in English those who are left-handed can't see the word as it is being written. Those who are right-handed may have the same problem when writing Hebrew.

Development and age when Hebrew learning begins will also have an effect on the children's awareness of direction. In some religious schools Hebrew language is introduced in the first grade using whole word recognition, without having to place letters in their right-to-left sequence. *For example*, areas and items around the room are labeled with their appropriate name and are referred to by their Hebrew name. It is a visual association and *not* a reading process. In general, until left to right is firmly established in English, it would not be a good idea to begin formal Hebrew learning with its conflicting elements.

Introduction of conversational Hebrew or learning prayer by rote may meet with much success in the younger grades. It will delight the child to be able to participate in the family Shabbat dinner or recite even a single line of the Ma Nishtana from memory at the family Pesach Seder—and this can occur long before a single word of Hebrew can be visually recognized.

STANDARDIZATION OF LETTERS

A most important factor in teaching Hebrew is to make sure that letters are standardized in shape and size and are kept consistent throughout the year. A problem arises, however, because there are many different typefaces in the various textbooks. In addition, Hebrew print in the prayerbook will most likely be different from the classroom text. These differences may seem slight to those who are familiar with the language, but these variations can cause much confusion and frustration to those who are just learning. The thickness and the angulation of the letters will differ from book to book. *Example:* ש ש ש. The shift from the vertical line could cause some children to think it's a different letter altogether. Therefore, when teaching the letters from a specific text it should be explained to the pupils that the letters have specific components which will always be there no matter what Hebrew book they are reading.* Having several books available with different typefaces for the students to see will illustrate this point.

In writing, a standard stick-figure letter may be easiest to learn because it corresponds closely with the printed letter in the text. It is also the easiest to write: ה ד ג ב א .

When, and at what stage, script is taught differs from temple to temple. We will not deal with this issue other than to say that for those children with learning disabilities the learning of script is more difficult since it requires manual dexterity and fine motor skill which may be a problem for specific children. The visual image of script is so different from the print that it is like learning a whole new alef-bet. Since one of the goals of our religious schools is that children be comfortable at services and with the prayerbook, the learning of print would seem to be sufficient for certain students.

Varying Techniques

Often the best way to learn something new is to have it repeated in a variety of ways: as the Hebrew letters are

---

*See Elaine Heavenrich, "The Hebrew Student as Teacher," *Compass* (UAHC), Fall 1977.

taught, try presenting Hebrew through the use of more than one modality.

1. For hands-on approaches, here is a short list of different textures which can be used to make letters. Using this tactile method, the children can touch and feel the letters while they see them. Some of the textures are smooth, and some are abrasive. Some children will prefer one over the other.
   a. Finger paint
   b. Felt
   c. Playdough or clay
   d. Elmer's Glue-All, dried
   e. Elmer's Glue-All, mixed with sand
   f. Sandpaper
   g. String glued onto paper
   h. Various other materials and cloths

   The teacher selects one or more textures to be used for a classroom activity as the letters are taught. The teacher can also provide the structure of a letter, standard in size and shape, printed in block form and drawn on a background of cardboard or heavy paper. The students may then cover it with the chosen texture or cut the letter out of the chosen fabric.

2. Grouping letters into the following categories is a good activity when learning Hebrew:
   a. Letters above the line
   b. Letters below the line
   c. Final letters
   d. Letters which look alike
   e. Letters which sound alike

At the beginning of the year, the teacher supplies a stack of Ditto sheets prepared with the letters. The students cut out sections of the sheet and use them like flashcards when grouping letters. These sheets can be used for a variety of activities throughout the year (and can reduce teacher work later on).

3. Another tactile exercise for learning Hebrew letters is tracing letter shapes from a template with the fingers. (A template is a pattern: the edges of the space guide the finger and the space that is left is the pattern; a raised letter on a background is another method used in tracing with the fingers. Textured cards were discussed earlier.) Some children see only the large differences in the letters and need to feel them to ''see'' the finer distinctions as those found in these pairs of letters:

ה/ח   א/צ   ג/נ   ו/ן   ו/ז

4. Another technique in teachers' repertoires is having students find a specific letter among several others and reproduce it. *For example*, the teacher holds up the flashcard of one letter while saying its name and sound. At their desks, students find its duplicate among their own flashcards and hold up the correct card while repeating the sound. This exercise is helpful because the students *see* the letter while they *hear* its sound. Or the teacher has all the students form a circle. Each student is given a large paper printed with a Hebrew letter. Only five or six *different* letters are used at one time, but there is a duplicate for each letter. At the signal, the students hold up their letters, look for their duplicate letters, and walk to their classmates holding the matching

letters. After all students have found their partners, the teacher checks all the pairs. (The first time this exercise is attempted, the teacher may well permit the children a little healthy bedlam. However, the children must then be returned to the more structured atmosphere of the activity.)

5. When introducing vocabulary, a similar technique can be used. The teacher holds up a picture card while saying the word; the image along with its sound helps the children to remember. The teacher does not ask the children to read it individually, aloud, in front of the class, but rather to find its duplicate at their desks. The children have only the words at their desks, not the pictures. The students' cards and the teacher's cards should correspond in size.

6. Felt boards and pocket charts are excellent educational aids for a Hebrew-language classroom. Pocket charts are used for organizing, categorizing, and matching pictures with words and also for sequencing words and letters. Felt boards can be used by each child, as well as by the teacher, during a demonstration in front of the class. For activity at the desk, the teacher or student aide cuts pieces of felt shaped like the selected word and sized to correspond with standard index cards either 3'' by 5'' or 5'' by 7''. *Example:* for the word שָׁלוֹם the individual felt boards are shaped like this . Using a different color, another piece of felt is used to cut out the block letters of *shin, lamed, vav, mem,*

including the dots and vowel. These letters and the small felt board are kept in an envelope along with an index card upon which the word שָׁלוֹם is written. When a child has difficulty with a word, the child is given the envelope. With the index card as the word model, and using the correct sequence of letters shown by the shape of the felt board, the child can reproduce the word. These envelopes can be filed and used as reference throughout the year.

7.   Along with felt boards, another way to teach spelling is by *closure. Example:* Have the child look at a word. Take away a letter. Have the child reproduce the missing letter, or find that letter which the teacher has placed among other letters. (The letters can be made from a variety of materials.)

PHONICS

Is it better to teach Hebrew by phonics or by whole-word recognition? Some children learn better one way, and some learn better another way. Using both approaches together may benefit the majority of the students.

Children who begin their Hebrew training when they are in the third grade have already spent two years reading their primary language, English. Many of the texts used in the elementary grades employ phonics techniques as the building blocks for reading. Thus there are children who expect, from their past experience with English, to learn the Hebrew letters individually and in various combinations. They look for the security of having the tools to build words with which to read, and for many phonics serves as this tool.

If the whole-word method is used alone, the children may feel lost because they cannot figure out words they haven't seen before. The whole-word method would be better utilized with children in nursery school and in kindergarten *before* they learn to read.

Therefore, when teaching Hebrew reading, it might benefit most students to follow the previously established learning approaches in their English language study. A basic alef-bet primer should be used with any whole-word text that is chosen for a particular grade. Phonics can be *more* easily taught in Hebrew than in English because the sound and its symbol have a predictable regularity. In Hebrew it is the vowel which directs the sound. A *shin* שׁ will always have the *sh* sound, but when *ay* is added to it, it makes *shay* שֵׁ. There are exceptions, such as that found in the word *luach* לוּחַ. When the *chet* comes at the end of the word, the vowel is pronounced first. Only the order is changed, *not* the sound of the letter.

ORAL LANGUAGE SKILLS

Children with a specific learning disability may learn one aspect of a language better than another. For example, the *oral* language may be successful for some children. These children can both remember spoken language directed to them as well as use it to speak to others. Yet these same students may have difficulty *reading* Hebrew. Visual recognition is a problem for them. They may need to learn Hebrew by rote or the teacher may have to use a sing-song voice when presenting Hebrew vocabulary. (A *good* tape recorder is an excellent tool for these children: Tapes are prepared for the children to listen to, and the children also tape and listen to themselves.) Since many children who have language problems (whether in English or in Hebrew) are able to learn music easily, chanted prayers can be taught even though the words cannot be read. Although they are frustrated in other areas of Hebrew learning, children who participate in prayer services—and who receive positive recognition for their participation from their families and peers—feel successful.

In general, when the letters are taught, their sounds—not their names—should be emphasized. *Example:* Say to the child, "This is the letter *lamed* and it has the sound *le.*" Have the child repeat the *le,* not the *lamed.* Many children will grasp both easily, but for some it will be confusing to have to remember the visual symbol and the sound of the symbol *and* its name because they do not exactly correspond.

LEARNING BY BODY MOVEMENT

In addition to the techniques previously discussed involving fine muscle coordination of the fingers and hand, we can help teach youngsters the Hebrew letters by using the larger muscles. *For example,* letters may be "written" in the air. This will require use of the whole arm. The game of "Stepping Stones" is also a good exercise involving the whole body. The teacher writes out letters or words on large pieces of paper and places them on the floor either in a line for walking on, or two-by-two for jumping on. As the children walk or jump onto the letters they call out the letter—either by sound or by name.

EDUCATIONAL AIDS

There are many educational aids for the teaching of Hebrew which the teacher can make to meet a specific classroom need. Wood letter blocks can be used in many ways. At a lumber store buy a square dowel or baluster which comes in various widths from 1 1/4 inches to 1 5/8 inches and which can be bought by the foot. Saw it into blocks about

2" by 5/8". Sand and then paint the Hebrew aleph-bet on them, one letter on a block. Divide the block into three imaginary parts. Do not divide the block with actual marks or lines because the students may become confused. The upper third is for the letter and is the largest space; the upper and middle-third space is large enough to accommodate a final letter. The bottom third is for the vowels. (The dotted lines here are for illustrative purposes only. The actual blocks do not have lines.)

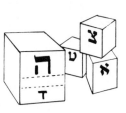

The vowels can be made of cardboard with double-sided adhesive tape on the back and placed on the bottom third when forming words. Although this is a project which requires extra time by the teacher, the blocks can be used for many activities, and remain in the classroom for years.* Because of the square shape, the corners are clearly defined and when placed together, letters will appear in proper visual alignment. Among the uses for the blocks are:

   a. building words
   b. practicing letter-vowel combinations
   c. practicing letter combinations
   d. building prayers
   e. learning prayers or sentences

Example: Write a prayer on a large paper using box shapes for the letters:

---

*The teacher can enlist the aid of parents or high school students from the religious school for this kind of project.

The students look among the blocks and place the correct block over the square with the corresponding letter. (A shoe box or wooden box which is divided into squares the same size as the blocks provides another kind of learning experience.)

Numerous ready-made educational games are available in Jewish bookstores. Among these we have chosen the following for their suitability:

a. Hebrew-letter pegboard set by Buki toys of Israel—good because the plastic letters are raised above the board and offer tactile experience.

b. Plastic snap-together colored Hebrew letters by KTAV—good because letters are in template form.

c. Rubber letters by Lauri—good because it offers textured surfaces that can be used as templates or as solid letters.

d. Alef-Bet Pick-Up sticks by KTAV—properly proportioned letter-size—that also can be placed in Styrofoam so they stay upright.

e. Twister game by KTAV—good because it involves the whole body.

f. Magnetic board alef-bet by KTAV—good for teaching spelling by closure—easy to move around.

g. Alef-Bet Stickums by KTAV—brightly printed ½'' plastic squares with adhesive backing—good for reinforcing letter identification and reading practice.

The more variety introduced into the Hebrew lessons, the more likely it is that the teacher will be meeting the specific needs of several individual students in the class. *Among those students may be children who do not have a learning disability but who do have problems specific to the learning of Hebrew.*

10

Bar/Bat Mitzvah:
Adaptations and Modifications

"...at least God knows I'm doing the best I can."

Quote from a Bar Mitzvah boy
with a learning disability.

BAR/BAT MITZVAH, MORE THAN ANY OTHER TIME IN A CHILD'S
Jewish education, encompasses and absorbs the entire family. The family becomes involved in the preparation of
festivities for the event as well as with the schedule of
Bar/Bat Mitzvah lessons. The Bar/Bat Mitzvah child then
carries the burden of living up to the standards set by both the
family and the congregation. Most children also place additional expectations upon themselves in response to the performances of friends who have already gone through their
Bar/Bat Mitzvah ceremonies. It is a time of expectation and
worry, of excitement and joy for all families with children
preparing for a Bar/Bat Mitzvah.

In families with children who are capable of preparing for
their Bar/Bat Mitzvah without additional help or time, and
who read Hebrew with fluency, many worries and anxieties
are avoided. But for the family with a child who has not
mastered the skills necessary for reading Hebrew (for example, a child who cannot learn using the visual recognition that
is usually needed when preparing for the Bar/Bat Mitzvah)

there can be tremendous tension. These parents often ask themselves, "Is my child going to make it?"

This chapter is addressed to the needs of these families and their Bar/Bat Mitzvah children. Along with their children, parents feel the extra burden of expectations for the Bar/Bat Mitzvah placed upon them by the extended family of grandparents and aunts and uncles, and by their friends. No one knows the impact of their child's learning problems better than the parents. They live with the problems every day and they try to understand. *But for the Bar/Bat Mitzvah preparation, many parents have difficulty accepting the problems they can—and do—accept at other times.* This time of preparation is an emotional one and parents often ask themselves: "Why can't my child be like everyone else just this once?" And in frustration they ask, "What are we going to do?" "Where can we turn for help?" Hopefully they will be able to turn to their temple for guidance and help so that at least some of these anxieties are relieved. What can the temple offer these families?

The rabbi is usually the person who supervises the form of Bar/Bat Mitzvah ceremonies and often is the person to whom the parents first go to discuss their concerns. It is a time when initial worries can be eased with alternative suggestions from the rabbi. Two such possibilities are:

A. Have the Bar/Bat Mitzvah on a Monday or Thursday morning when the format is different and the service is shortened, instead of on the usual Shabbat time. This change allows for modifications in the structure of the service, and because the congregants are less familiar with services at this time, they are likely unaware of modifications and changes.

B. Have the Bar/Bat Mitzvah during a holiday when the

Torah is brought out to be read and when the format of the service is completely different than that followed on the Shabbat. In this way many modifications could be made for the child and since there is no rigid format to follow, the congregation will not be expecting a specific Torah service.

But what about the parents who keep their worries to themselves and do not go to the rabbi (or anyone else at the temple)? Their general inability to accept the fact that their child has a learning problem is so strong they convince themselves that for the Bar/Bat Mitzvah everything will "turn out just fine." And much of the time it does, but at the expense of the family's well-being and the child's increasingly negative feelings about Bar/Bat Mitzvah. In such instances the religious school can play a part in helping the child. This is most effectively done if the parents voluntarily approach the subject. However, as previously stated, they may feel much inhibition regarding their mixed feelings about Bar/Bat Mitzvah and their child. Perhaps one way to deal with this is to check *each* child's religious school records prior to Bar/Bat Mitzvah training to ascertain if there was any previous learning problem. The religious school gives the background of the child's learning problem to the person preparing the Bar/Bat Mitzvah lessons. Modifications now used in the classroom are included. With this advance information, some modifications could be prepared and applied when the child first comes for individual lessons.

Fortunately for the boy who was quoted at the beginning of the chapter, positive feelings toward Judaism already existed as a part of his life, long before the Bar Mitzvah day approached. Lines were deleted from the Torah portion to help him finish his preparation in time. No matter how hard he tried he couldn't handle the length of the portion *along with all the other prayers* he needed to learn as part of the service. It didn't upset him, however. In his heart *he* knew God would accept his Torah reading on his Bar Mitzvah day.

It is helpful to have the rabbi explain to parents and children that *it is a common procedure* to take lines out of Bar/Bat Mitzvah portions after they are assigned and that this is done for many children for many reasons. *No one in the congregation has a scorecard and no one is counting the total number of lines read from the Torah. This kind of explanation is important so that the children can feel that their Bar/Bat Mitzvah is as valid as anyone else's.*

The following are modifications which help children who cannot learn their Bar/Bat Mitzvah service as it is usually structured:

1. The quantity of Hebrew which exists in the Torah and Haftarah portions and in the surrounding prayers which accompany the service can seem a staggering amount to the child who has difficulty reading Hebrew. The answer for this child is simply to shorten the amount both in the number of lines of the portion and in the amount of prayers to be read by the child at the service. In certain instances this need can be anticipated and the child is given a shortened portion to begin with.

2. Allow for some prayers to be read in English, and a major section of the Torah portion to be read in English with only a few lines read in Hebrew. Where necessary, these lines could be learned by rote rather than by reading.

3. Some children who find learning to read or speak Hebrew difficult find it easier to learn Hebrew when

music is involved. Therefore Hebrew which is chanted (as in the Haftarah) and the blessings immediately preceding and following the Torah and Haftarah meet with much success. The Torah portion could be read in English; the rest of the Torah service could be learned without additional modifications.

4. Some children panic when they are asked to speak or to appear before a classroom of peers. It is extremely difficult for them to appear before an entire congregation. In such instances the rabbi or cantor could softly chant and read along with the child. Sometimes having this supporting adult standing next to the Bar/Bat Mitzvah child will be all that is necessary to give assurance that help is at hand if it is needed. This may be more easily done on a day other than Shabbat when the format could easily be structured differently. In some severe cases when a child simply cannot handle the fear of being in front of the congregation, a Bar/Bat Mitzvah service at home with family and friends is another option. Many times throughout Jewish history Jews have prayed in their homes and not at the temple. Many small congregations are doing so today.

5. Reading transliteration rather than the Hebrew itself is a help to some children. However the unfamiliar combination of English letters in nonsense syllables can be confusing and just as difficult as reading the Hebrew. It is of some help *with certain words and phrases,* and there are children who do feel comfortable using a limited amount of transliteration.

6. In many temples with large congregations it may be

impossible to schedule a single Bar/Bat Mitzvah for a particular Shabbat service. However, this must be considered for the child who has a learning problem. If that child is paired with someone who reads well and has learned the service easily, the child with the problem may feel inadequate or feel that people are making comparisons, or that the performance doesn't measure up to what the other child is doing. Scheduling the Bar/Bat Mitzvah either as a "single " or on a weekday would be good for these children.

7. It is helpful to some children to have their Bar/Bat Mitzvah later than their thirteenth year. This additional maturation time helps the child to better handle the many aspects of preparing for Bar/Bat Mitzvah. It is not necessarily a modification that would cause either the child or the child's peers to question, particularly if it is presented as a matter of scheduling.

The following are suggestions which can be built into the Bar/Bat Mitzvah lessons:

1. The Bar/Bat Mitzvah teacher should merely introduce all the parts of the Torah service which the Bar/Bat Mitzvah student is required to learn. (These parts already may have been modified.) Often a student is introduced to and taught the Torah portion first. When that is learned, the Haftarah is introduced, then the prayers, etc. Just when the child feels the satisfaction of completion, a new element is brought in! The student begins to feel frustrated—what has been learned is never enough! *When the whole service is shown to the student at the beginning of the lessons, the student knows what to expect and can strive for completion.*

2. After the required Torah service and prayers are introduced, the various elements of the service are broken into small sections to be learned one part at a time. One way to do this is by visual chunking. As was explained earlier, *chunking* applies to the amount of subject matter a child can handle at one time. *Visual chunking* refers to the number of words or lines the child sees and learns at a time.

   a. For some children, the limit will be only one or two words to see and learn at one time. For other children, one or two lines will be easily handled.

   b. It is difficult for some children to focus on the words and lines of the portion because they are spaced too closely. Cut out the lines from a Xerox copy and, leaving more space between each line, tape them on cardboard.

   c. To help focus attention on the line being read, have the child slide a card or ruler down the page as each line is read.

   d. Have the child practice reading with the *yad* (Torah pointer), Judaism's built-in helper.

   e. Visually divide the Torah portion according to the number of *aliyot*. The child then sees and has an image of the exact amount to read before stopping for an *aliyah*.

   f. The *trop* in both the Torah and Haftarah is used to show the reader how the words are chanted. These markings are placed with the words and look much like vowels. For the child who is already having difficulty with reading Hebrew letters and vowels, this can be another distraction causing even more confusion and frustration. Rewrite the Torah portion without the *trop.*

3. If a child has to learn primarily through sound, the parts of the Torah service can be broken into *auditory chunking.*

   a. Words may have to be broken down, a syllable at a time, to be heard and repeated.

   b. Lines may have to be broken down to listening and repeating, a few words at a time, until the child feels that more can be added.

4. It is common for the Bar/Bat Mitzvah teacher to make tapes of the Torah and Haftarah portions as well as the prayers. This is a great help to some students because they can regulate the amount to be learned at their own speed. Other students do better *without* use of a tape, and teachers should be aware of these individual reactions.

5. Children with learning problems may require extra time to prepare for Bar/Bat Mitzvah. A decision on when Bar/Bat Mitzvah preparations should begin will have to be made for each child; the length of each lesson is also decided on an individual basis.

   For some children an additional month or two and longer lesson periods—planned for from the beginning—may be the single most important modification.

6. Bar/Bat Mitzvah lessons are more helpful on a one-to-one basis than those held in a class of Bar/Bat Mitzvah students. This alleviates distractions as well as the worry of comparison with other Bar/Bat Mitzvah children.

7. After the Bar/Bat Mitzvah lessons are well on their way, the child may become less concerned with the *content of the service* and begin to worry about the

details of the performance. As soon as that begins to concern the child, make the time to take care of it even though other children might not have that worry in this point of their preparation.

At such time, have the child attend a Bar/Bat Mitzvah service to see the actual details (when to walk to the ark, when to hold the Torah, when to sit down, etc.). It is also helpful to have the child "walk through" the sequence of events on the *bimah* when the sanctuary is empty.

8. Prior to the actual service, a good review for the Bar/Bat Mitzvah student is to tape the entire Torah service. Included in this tape is the child's own explanation of what is happening during each part of the service. *Example:* "Now that I've read the Torah portion and said the blessings, I walk to the chair behind the *bimah* and wait for the rabbi." In this way the Bar/Bat Mitzvah child rehearses every step that takes place on Bar/Bat Mitzvah day. Hopefully, as the tape is played back, the child will develop a sense of security that things will go well. This tape can also be used to send to a relative who might not be able to attend the service. The making of such a tape is a mitzvah in itself.

9. When parents come to pick up their child, the Bar/Bat Mitzvah teacher should describe their child's progress. It would be a great help to them. A word or two emphasizing what the child does well will ease some of the parents' anxiety. What the child cannot do and still needs to work on should also be expressed, but the words of encouragement will certainly help alleviate the tension and worry which goes along with Bar/Bat Mitzvah preparation.

A note of caution: Modifications in the Bar/Bat Mitzvah ceremony should be subtle. Modifications that will be readily apparent to those in the congregation *must be acceptable to the student*. When the occasion is over, it is critically important to the Bar/Bat Mitzvah celebrant that it was a true success and not just a successful second-rate "performance" considering that "I'm not as good as the other kids." Some students with learning disabilities have turned down efforts at modifications and by carrying out the service without change have surpassed the expectations of their families and teachers. *It is unwise to force modification upon any student who is motivated to do otherwise.*

We have purposely saved the discussion of the Bar/Bat Mitzvah child for last. Why? To show that the concerns of the adults are sometimes so overwhelming that the feelings and worries of the child are often overlooked. But here we have a Bar Mitzvah boy and a Bat Mitzvah girl. What is going on in their heads during this flurry of activity and preparation concerning them? What are they thinking about? These children have certainly picked up the anxieties which the adults around them project. And certainly they have picked up any questions by the adults concerning their own ability to do well. But there are other worries which are particular to these children.

At the adolescent age of Bar/Bat Mitzvah, peer pressure is very strong. The Bar Mitzvah boy and the Bat Mitzvah girl are well aware of how their peers react to a good "performance" or to a mistake. They themselves have sat as part of the congregation and made their own remarks when a friend was on the bimah. This worries them now!

For these children even oral participation in the classroom is torture, yet they know they have to go through with the Bar/Bat Mitzvah ceremony. This worries them!

Let us as educators and parents show our children that we care about their feelings. Let us show them that there are means available to help them be successful. Let us show them that the Bar/Bat Mitzvah ceremony can be a fulfilling religious experience for *every* child.

11

Standards and Evaluations
in the Religious School

THUS FAR WE HAVE DISCUSSED VARIOUS MODIFICATIONS AND
changes which can be applied to teaching in the individual
classroom. But what about modifications in the overall goals
of the religious school? Are the requirements and standards
realistic and equally applicable to all the students? It is entirely possible to make modifications and yet to *maintain a
respect for standards.* Relaxing standards or allowing for
flexibility does not mean throwing out requirements. What it
does necessitate is establishing and working toward standards
and requirements that fit the child and that work in a larger
sense toward the broader goals of the religious school.

What about the sixth-grade child who is reading at fourth-
grade level? How is that child going to finish the amount of
work required by the standards of that sixth-grade curriculum? No matter how many modifications are made, that
child is still going to read at fourth-grade level. That child
probably has accomplished something worthwhile as a Jew
during that year, but in no way can that child be expected to
meet the predetermined standards for sixth grade—the simple

reason is that child *cannot* meet them! And how can the child who could only handle two years of Hebrew meet a four-year requirement necessary to begin Bar/Bat Mitzvah preparation? Can we penalize that child as a Jew and say there will be no Bar/Bat Mitzvah?

Part of the answer comes from the input and understanding of the parent, the rabbi, the teacher, the principal, and the school committee: Are they ready to meet the needs of individual students? Are they willing to accept work in a student's own best learning style? Is the school committee ready to grab hold of a child in need? Just as Tevya the Milkman, faced with difficult questions concerning his daughters, tried to accept new and unfamiliar ideas—so must we bend to help our Jewish children with learning problems. The Jewish child living in twentieth-century America is confronted by the demands of Judaism as communicated by the religious school. Stress resulting from frustration in attempting to meet religious school requirements often leads the child to break away from religious school altogether.

At some point you, as a teacher, may be in conflict with yourself: "How can I grade this child?" Perhaps you question a negative remark you considered writing on a student's paper, or you question the work you ask of the class. The questioning and conflict represent the beginning of understanding individual students. A search for answers can begin. Can you consider modifying your own standards in the classroom? Can you find ways other than the usual pencil-and-paper testing system to evaluate students? Perhaps you can utilize such options as:

1. Taking time to listen to a tape of a child's answer *instead of* a written report.
2. Accepting a picture accompanied by an oral report *instead of* a written report.

3. Accepting three written answers *instead of* eight.
4. Correcting for content *instead of* spelling and grammar.
5. Taking time to make an organization chart or materials for students to categorize *instead of* a written exam.
6. Taking time to listen to a child deliver an oral exam privately *instead of* as part of the class.

By testing children according to their individual abilities it becomes possible to give them grades based upon their own style of learning. A grade has much more meaning to a child when it is given with an understanding of the child's growth and achievement.

The principal and the school committee can work with the teacher and give the support needed to experiment with ways of testing and evaluating students according to specific needs of individuals. They must all work together to develop standards and requirements in overall goals for each grade level that will apply to the individuals within each grade. These requirements and standards can take the form of flexible guidelines which allow the latitude necessary in trying to meet individual needs. The only fixed requirement should be to provide the religious background and Jewish identity which will be meaningful to individual students as Jews.

Conclusion

THE PURPOSE OF THIS BOOK IS TO PRESENT AN APPROACH TO Jewish religious education which focuses on the child with specific individual needs. It is not our intent to provide answers. It is our intent to provide a means for creatively questioning and creatively searching for answers to meet these needs. The responsibility for meeting these needs lies in the hands of many people:

Parents must be willing to come forward and to share valuable information about their children with the religious school and must realize that their input can help their children to greater appreciate and love our Jewish heritage.

Teachers must develop the ability to "see" students and to be confident in their observations. They must be willing to try and try again; to understand that what works well for one child may not work at all for another; to appreciate that lessons and activities are not going to be 100 percent successful for every child at every lesson; and to recognize that modifications tailored to meet the needs of one particular student may well benefit others.

The *principal and school committee,* aware of their important roles as intermediaries between the classroom teacher and outside sources, must be willing to create new and flexible standards so that students may learn in their own ways about their religious heritage. They must realize that their willingness to be flexible may well be the key to a child's continuing Judaism.

If religious school personnel are inexperienced in communicating with outside sources, the forms suggested in this book may be used to begin the first steps in communication. Through the information received from outside sources and from personal observations, it is possible to become sensitive to what students are able to do, and to then capitalize on those strengths when planning lessons.

We ask those teachers, rabbis, principals, and school committees who have already prepared successful programs in their classrooms and schools to share your ideas with your colleagues...there are so many modifications and guidelines yet to be invented.

Let us keep in mind our long-range objectives: We want to provide a religious education which will help make our children knowledgeable Jews and to create a Jewish environment which will involve each individual personally.

This book began with a question: *How is Judaism going to cope with Jewish children with learning differences?* It will close with another: *Are we now ready to deal with the problems of those children who are questions in search of answers?*

Suggested Readings

1. Assistance to States for Education of Handicapped Children. *Federal Register.* Vol. 42, No. 250, Dec. 29, 1977.
2. Berman, B. The Logistics of Learning Centers, *Alternatives in Religious Education.* Winter, 1977.
3. Cruickshank, W. and Johnson, G.O. (Eds.). *Education of Exceptional Children and Youth,* 3rd edition. Englewood Cliffs, N.J.: Prentice Hall, 1975.
4. Education of Handicapped Children. *Federal Register.* Vol. 42, No. 163, Aug. 23, 1977.
5. Gibson, E.J. and Levin, H. *The Psychology of Reading.* Cambridge: MIT Press, 1975.
6. Goodman, L. and Mann, L. *Learning Disabilities in the Secondary School, Issues and Practices.* New York: Grune and Stratton, 1976.
7. Haring, N.G. (Ed.) *Behavior of Exceptional Children, An Introduction to Special Education.* Columbus, Ohio: Chas. E. Merritt, 1974.
8. Harris, A. and Sipay, E.R. *How to Increase Reading Ability,* 6th edition. New York: David McKay, 1975.
9. Heavenrich, E. "The Hebrew Student as Teacher." *Compass* (UAHC), Fall 1977.
10. Hewitt, F.M. with Forness, S.R. *Education of Exceptional Learners,* 2nd edition. Boston: Allyn and Bacon, 1977.
11. Jansky, J. and de Hirsch, K. *Preventing Reading Failure.* New York: Harper and Row, 1972.

12. Johnson, D. and Myklebust, H. *Learning Disabilities, Educational Principles and Practices.* New York: Grune and Stratton, 1967.

13. Kephart, N.C. *The Slow Learner in the Classroom.* Columbus, Ohio: Chas. E. Merrill, 1971.

14. Kirk, S.A. *Educating Exceptional Children,* 2nd edition. Boston: Houghton Mifflin, 1972.

15. Ledgin, R. Set Your Own Pace in Hebrew Learning Centers, *Alternatives in Religious Education.* Winter 1977.

16. Lerner, J.W. *Children with Learning Disabilities, Theories, Diagnosis, and Teaching Strategies,* 2nd edition. Boston: Houghton Mifflin, 1976.

17. McCarthy, J.J. and McCarthy, J.F. *Learning Disabilities.* Boston: Allyn and Bacon Inc., 6th printing, 1972.

18. Mordock, J.B. *The Other Children, An Introduction to Exceptionality.* New York: Harper and Row, 1975.

19. Myers, P.I. and Hammill, D.D. *Methods for Learning Disorders,* 2nd edition. New York: J.C. Wiley, 1976.

20. Smith, J.A. *Creative Teaching of the Language Arts in the Elementary School.* Boston: Allyn and Bacon, 1974.

21. Smith, Sally L. *No Easy Answers, The Learning Disabled Child.* DHEW Publications, 1978. For sale by the Superintendent of Documents, U.S. Printing Office, Washington, D.C.

22. Wallace, G. and Kauffman, J.M. *Teaching Children with Learning Problems.* Columbus, Ohio: Chas. E. Merrill, 1973.

23. Wallace, G. and McLoughlin, J. *Learning Disabilities, Concepts and Characteristics.* Columbus, Ohio: Chas. E. Merrill, 1975.

About the Authors

ROBERTA M. GREENE brings a wealth of experience to this volume—as an elementary school teacher, as an education editor with Houghton Mifflin Company, as a special education tutor, and as an educational consultant who is well familiar with observation, diagnosis, and remediation of children with learning disabilities.

Ms. Greene, a member of Temple Beth Shalom in Needham, Massachusetts, has served on its school committee and was chairperson of the religious school board for two years. The teacher-sensitization seminars she helped plan and conduct for religious school personnel there led to the development of *A Question in Search of an Answer.*

Author of the children's book, *Two and Me Makes Three* (selected by the Child Study Children's Book Committee of The Bank Street School for inclusion in its anthology, *Friends Are Like That*), Roberta Greene holds a B.S. degree in Early Childhood Education from Syracuse University, an Ed.M. degree from Harvard Graduate School of Education, and is currently completing doctoral studies in the Program in Applied Psycholinguistics of Boston University School of Education.

At present, Ms. Greene is conducting research in problems of social perception associated with learning disorder.

ELAINE HEAVENRICH is an experienced pedagogic supervisor and classroom teacher. She has worked with students of all ages—primary through high school—in a variety of educational settings that also includes coordinator of Jewish programming in camp environments.

Ms. Heavenrich has developed materials and strategies for teaching both those children in her classes who have learning disabilities and those she has tutored in Hebrew studies and Bar/Bat Mitzvah preparation.

At Temple Beth Shalom, Needham, Massachusetts, she was teacher liaison to the school committee and was instrumental in helping to create the junior high school curriculum. Her feature article, "The Hebrew Student As Teacher," appeared in *Compass* magazine, Fall 1977.

Elaine Heavenrich is currently a member of the religious school staff of Temple Beth El, Birmingham, Michigan; is tutoring students in Hebrew language; and is working toward her master's degree in special education at Wayne State University in Detroit, Michigan.

DR. JANET W. LERNER is currently professor of Special Education at Northeastern Illinois University, Chicago, Illinois. She earned her Ph.D. at New York University. Dr. Lerner has worked as an elementary classroom teacher, as a reading specialist in elementary and secondary schools, as a teacher of brain-injured children, and as a college instructor. Her college teaching includes City College of the City University of New York, National College of Education, Northwestern University, and Northeastern Illinois University. She is the author of numerous articles, chapters, and books. Her book, *Children with Learning Disabilities: Theories, Diagnosis, and Teaching Strategies*, which is currently in its second edition, won the Pi Lamda Theta award in 1973 for one of the twenty-four outstanding books of the year in the field of education. Dr. Lerner serves on several boards including the Professional Advisory Board of the Association for Children with Learning Disabilities, treasurer of the Division for Children with Learning Disabilities in the Council for Exceptional Children, and the Commission on Jewish Education of the Union of American Hebrew Congregations and the Central Conference of American Rabbis. The Association for Children with Learning Disabilities selected Dr. Lerner for its highest award, its ACLD award in 1978.

Commission on Jewish Education
of the
Union of American Hebrew Congregations
and
Central Conference of American Rabbis

UNION EDUCATION SERIES
Edited by
DANIEL B. SYME, *National Director of Education*

Director of Publications
Stuart L. Benick